D1432417

HOW YOU CAN COMMAND RESPECT AND BE LOVED FOR IT

KNOWLEDGE AND SKILLS
TO CHANGE YOUR LIFE

JAMES TAYLOR

iUniverse, Inc.
New York   Bloomington

HOW YOU CAN COMMAND RESPECT
AND BE LOVED FOR IT
KNOWLEDGE AND SKILLS TO
CHANGE YOUR LIFE

iUniverse books may be ordered through booksellers or by contacting:

iUniverse
1663 Liberty Drive
Bloomington, IN 47403
www.iuniverse.com
1-800-Authors (1-800-288-4677)

Because of the dynamic nature of the Internet, any Web addresses or links
contained in this book may have changed since publication and may no longer be
valid. The views expressed in this work are solely those of the author and do not
necessarily reflect the views of the publisher, and the publisher hereby disclaims
any responsibility for them.

ISBN: 978-1-4502-0841-3 (pbk)
ISBN: 978-1-4502-0842-0 (ebook)

Printed in the United States of America

iUniverse rev. date: 1 / 23 / 10

Contents

INTRODUCTION

This book is intended to look at the aspects of social improvement which will be of most interest to the reader, these I think are probably -

1. The way people see us and what we can do to make people give us a 'high score' when they meet us.
2. The best ways to handle situations which are 'diplomatically challenging'.
3. The 'switches' we can use to enhance our powers of PERSUASION.
4. The 'switches' we can use to enhance our powers of ATTRACTION.
5. The things we can do to increase our PRESENCE.
6. The things we can do to enhance our SOCIAL STATUS.
7. How can we be seen as the person everyone loves.

Curiously, on the surface you would imagine the whole set to come as a package, but though this is largely so, the ingredients for some aspects of the equation can almost contradict the ingredients for others. For example if we look at 4 and compare it to 7, I'm sure we all know of some people we are attracted to but don't consider loveable people. Also if we compare 2 and compare it to 6, I expect you could think of a number of people who are high in social status who lack diplomacy!

The answer to this paradox is JUDGEMENT. If you want to perform to your optimum as a person you need to know when it is most appropriate to adopt the qualities which are most appropriate to the situation you are in. There are many aspects of social wisdom, and if you think around people you know you will notice how different people have particular skills in certain areas. In fact, as a quick exercise now, scan down the list and see which people you can think of have particular talents for each of the 7 skills mentioned. You now have 7 different role models for these skills! In order to have the ultimate social dexterity we want to have a mastery of all of these skills, and we want to have good judgement in order to flow from one skill to the other whenever it is appropriate to do this. This book will give you all of the details you need on what these switches are, and it is up to you to use your good judgement and to develop the ability to recognise where each is appropriate.

CHAPTER 1

How am I doing at the moment?

It's almost impossible to see yourself in the way others would see you – for one thing everyone sees you differently and through their own 'filters', and as a second problem you are you and you can't step outside your own body – even when you watch yourself on video you will be seeing yourself through your own 'filters' and you will probably see just about everything you did as fitting behaviour for the given situation. If you've ever sat and people watched you will know that you can get an amazing amount of information about a person in a few seconds – you could take a fair guess at their job, intelligence, nationality, wealth, level of confidence, social skills and a whole lot more. How do you think these people might see YOU? Remember they will all have their own unique filters, so do your best to take on their particular filters as you do this!

One thing you can do is to look for people who you would consider similar to yourself and examine your feelings towards THEM. Do you like them? I hope you do! Well now, let's take a quick look at the sort of criteria you might have used to 'size someone up' in that initial glance.

1. Their general posture, they may be confidently upright or they may be bent over and curled up.
2. The angle of their head, it could be forward and looking at the ground or it could be confidently upright, it might even be arrogantly bolt upright and slightly back!
3. Their facial expressions.
4. The speed of their movement.
5. Any gestures we see them doing.
6. The clothes they are wearing.
7. The way they walk.

This really is just about all that there is in that initial glance. Use this list to help you to gauge how people might see YOU.

Now then, it is interesting though how some people seem to totally lack charisma or presence until they TALK. Speech is a highly complex form of communication and there are many variable factors, but a clear speaking voice communicating eloquently is one of the most effective ingredients in the list of status raising attributes. Next time you hear your voice in a video playback assess it honestly. Remember that regional accent is not necessarily of importance, what IS important is that you have a clear voice with a pleasant tone which communicates effectively and fluently. As this book progresses we will look at both your posture and your voice in quite a bit of detail, looking at what we can do to make these as good as we can.

What do I really want?

One of the reasons you have bought this book is because you want to be more powerful socially -you want people to seek out your approval and advice more, and to value your presence and your words very highly. As this is closely linked with attraction we will 'shine a torch' in this direction a lot of the time. Let's chat about this.

Let's face it, what most of us really want is to be socially powerful -we want respect. To this end, people are buying books about persuasion, influence, leadership, and even hypnosis, all looking for that magic formula to 'push people's buttons' in order to make them like us, make them respect us, and above all to get them to 'do as we say'.

Although I will talk in great depth about the things we can do to make us more likeable, understanding and more loved, I will also talk about the things we can do to give us more 'presence' which is tied in with social status. This is slightly more 'edgy' stuff!

A lot of the things I might suggest to the effect of increasing your social power appear to recommend you to be just a little less involved with people, sometimes non empathetic, and to do some things which may or may not be seen as being a little mean (many of the things might make you less likeable, but paradoxically more popular). What I am doing is to offer to you the qualities I see as those of social status on an animal level, and a lot of these qualities aren't particularly likeable, but a knowledge of exactly what they are could go a long way. I would not for one minute suggest that you change your responses towards people dramatically, but I feel an understanding of the processes which are going on could make an IMMENSE difference to your life, and just knowing this stuff will be helpful even if you don't use it, as having a wider knowledge of these behaviours in itself will give you more confidence. I am hoping that you will read a lot of this and think 'aha, so that's what was happening when … … '

A good raid of the self help books shelf will give you a lot of ideas on how to be a nice and likeable person, and how to influence people through being a person who is respected and holds authority. A couple of books suggest the complete opposite and 'bastard' type behaviour, and of course they are all quite right within the contexts provided, so why is it that so many people have read book after book and maybe done a few courses and they still don't see the results they so desperately seek ? Will any of this work for YOU? Maybe the answer is that all the successful people who are discussed and used as models ALREADY had leadership qualities and were of high 'animal level' status, and the social awareness or ruthlessness, though connected with their success, in reality just became just part of their overall strategy. So where can we look to find out exactly what these magical qualities ARE which they already had? What exactly is it that gave these people this high status?

Okay, so what is a leader and what makes him or her different? Let's move away from human interaction and see where this might take us.

In many of the higher species of mammals, particularly those more closely related to the human species, there is usually a leader of the group - the alpha male. He is the one the others turn to for protection, the females turn to him for love, (well sex anyway!) and all of the group will turn to him for leadership!! He is not necessarily the strongest or the most striking male in the group, but he will possess certain qualities which make him the most respected in the group. Let's see what qualities an alpha male might have in the 'human' world, and let's say that in the human world these equate to STATUS AND LEADERSHIP qualities, tied up with social status, and are qualities which increase social value and social power .They can be seen as leadership behaviours and qualities of leadership rather than gender related characteristics, and as such would be just as effectively applied to a female leader. (alpha male and alpha female). These will give us a few more clues about what will work for us. Let's see how this model might work!

1. People turn to him/her for leadership and respect him, probably frequently seeking his/her advice and seeking his/her approval.

2. Tied in with (1), people seek protection from him/her, through her strong leadership those under her control will feel 'protected' from forces outside the group (maybe also protected from forces inside the group).

3. As a leader he will be 'in demand' and will be socially both more adept and more adaptable than his/her 'beta male/female' competitors, so he will be able to connect with other people at many different levels.

4. He/she may possess knowledge or skill, making them something of an authority within their chosen field (also tied in with (1)).

5. He/she might have great financial wealth, this may increase respect. Potential generosity further enhances this! Also wealth may induce others to feel envy, which is a very 'beta male' quality, which serves to emphasise the alpha qualities of the person possessing wealth.

6. He/she will be non-needy. After all, if they seek approval or advice they are acknowledging that someone else is in charge Of course, in the human world it usually IS a good idea to show respect for someone HIGHER up the ladder !

7. He/she will be confident in their abilities as leader and able to handle 'challengers' .They will probably be totally unperturbed by any challenger as they are accustomed to being challenged and they know how to handle these situations with ease.

8. Other people are seen to be looking to this person for leadership already, causing others to 'follow suite'.

9. Confident body language, taking up space and commanding a greater social distance during general interactions.

10. Emotional intelligence and first rate communication skills. Able to inspire other people with words and give speeches which people connect with.

11. A strong personality which is in control of the situation all of the time. In control of self and never over-responding to things. Certainly never panicking as this places control in the hands of those around him/her. (Panic transfers control) -He/she 'never lets them see him sweat', maybe a touch of James Bond !!

12. An overall personality which radiates authority and strong leadership, confidence in judgement, and strong speech which can override others in a combination of articulation, content and in some cases also volume.

So this is our animal leadership equation. Some people seem to be born with certain qualities, they seem to effortlessly become leaders of groups at school and go on to become leader personalities in adult life, getting all the good things in life with relative ease. We have to ask why this is. Think of a person at school who was highly charismatic.

1. were they more socially skilled?

Probably but not necessarily. Being a leader gave them a bit of an edge as others in the group were at least slightly focussed on competing with each other for the leader's approval, so they were less focussed on connecting with each other. The fact that they were competing only went to serve as 'proof' to everyone else of the high status of the leader. The leader meanwhile had a 'bird's eye view' of the social interactions around him/her.

2. Did they show interest in everyone else ?

When they showed interest in someone in the group there was probably an almost teacher/pupil dynamic going on. The person in the group felt decidedly honoured, though the leader probably showed them only a little bit of fairly superficial interest.

3. Did they have an understanding and magnanimous attitude?

Unlikely! Their attitude was probably one of strong self belief rather than one of working for the common good of the group. Ironically they probably made many wrong decisions but because their self-belief appeared to be so unshakeable they were always able to persuade others to follow them, and others just appeared to follow like sheep!

4. Did they stand out from the crowd in any obvious way?

Likely yes in one of these ways
  a) They were bigger and stronger - (esp. in male groups).
  b) They were the most aggressive - (esp. in male groups).
  c) They were louder and talked more.

    d) They had knowledge which was essential for the group to have.

    e) They were prettier- (female groups).

They had at least one of these five qualities and were probably envied for these qualities by others in the group.

5. How did YOU feel when you spoke to them?

Probably slightly intimidated and envious, respectful

6. How did they feel when they spoke to you?

They probably felt they were doing you a favour!

7. What other features did you notice?

They likely spoke more fluently (always clear and un-hurried) and tended to talk more than the others, having voices which seemed to just dominate the group. They had relatively upright posture and they seemed to be more aware of what was going on. Some members of the group were happy to just sit back while the leader took responsibility for a task, while at other times the leader might have delegated certain tasks. Generally they possessed a very 'proud' attitude, tipping over into arrogance, and used this unshakeable confidence to lead.

8. Anything else important?

Well yes, one of the most important things you notice is that they make solid decisions quickly. They might make wrong decisions but they are solid decisions stemming from reasonably good judgement. This speed of delivery of a decision managed to catch other people out as they were still thinking things through, and the leaders confident and assertive delivery of their decision could 'derail' other people who had they been allowed time to think things through their way may even have made better decisions.

Before we press on, just remember anyone you ever felt envy towards, or jealousy, and you'll notice how these emotions generated a curious attraction. If someone ignores you or is a bit 'stand offish' towards you a similar effect is triggered. Curious, isn't it!

So, looking at the two sets of qualities you can see that the 'alpha male of the group' properties are actually similar in fundamental dynamics to the properties which gave young Sharon or Kevin that popularity at school. Now let's take a look at the alpha male type of figure which pick up artists use as a model to draw ideas from. These are the main 'alpha characteristics' which will make a man attractive to a woman.

1. Appearing to have qualities of leadership through organising people. He might be a boss, or just the main man in a group. People respect him and seek his approval, maybe coming to seek his advice on various important issues.
2. Having status through knowledge. Again a leadership quality as people will come to him to seek his advice and approval. He may

have specialised knowledge as in the case of a Teacher or Doctor, or he may be a guru of some description.

3.   Having social intelligence. Knowing a lot of people and being liked and looked up to socially. Being socially 'in demand'. Being able to connect with many people on a range of different levels.

4.   Having a strong personality, knowing his own mind. Independent and not easily led, possibly to the extent of being arrogant.

5.   Protecting family, friends and loved ones. Having strongly held values - (much the same as

6.   Being non-needy and relatively un-reactive in situations where others might react, again this is closely linked to 4. Interestingly this is a quality which women test a lot at all stages of a relationship, in fact generally women consider any neediness to be a 'turn off' .

7.   Confident persona, ability to 'put a woman in her place'. Totally un-phased by a woman of extreme beauty as he is accustomed to having beautiful women around him.

8.   Pre-selection by other women. If a man is seen to be in a relationship with a woman who is considered highly attractive he will automatically be seen as a high status male – he has already been 'tested and selected'. Particularly he will be seen as very attractive by women who consider themselves less attractive than the lady he is with.

9. Confident masculine body language and vocal tonality. He takes up space and his sound is deep and relaxed.
10. Able to communicate well. Maybe telling stories which draw people in and lead the imagination. Able to emotionally connect. Able to lead other peoples' thoughts with these connecting and storytelling abilities.
11. An overall alpha attitude. Happy, cheeky. A bit full of himself, full of self confidence and possessing high self esteem.

All these qualities again relate to animal qualities, yet they are still the most important selection criteria (generally) in the mating game. Many of these qualities are more an attitude than learned behaviour, an attitude which reflects confidence, both general confidence and sexual confidence.

In addition to these alpha qualities there are certain non alpha qualities which women find a turn off, for example the nervous laugh, self qualification, submissive whining and complaining. In addition to women finding these a turn off, note that they are the very same qualities which will rapidly lower your social value male OR female (although a woman may well use a seductive giggle if she is giving a 'come on' to a man she perceives to be of high value).

The psychology of seduction has made fantastic advances over the last few years, and the chart above will illustrate just how similar the 'alpha behaviours' they seek to display in order to seduce are to those needed to raise our social value and command even more respect, and you can see just how relevant advances in seduction are in our quest for social status. Many of their ideas can be transferred almost directly from one field to the other !

When a person with leadership qualities interacts with a person of lower status we see a number of interesting things as an observer. From a distance it is possible to tell who is the leader and who isn't from the body language alone. Also there are many many conversational 'games' which are played by a leader, with certain things he would say and certain things he wouldn't say, and in the same way there are a number of things which a leader would do and some he wouldn't do. The things that a leader will say and do are called 'demonstrations of high value' (DHVs) and the things a leader would not do are referred to as 'demonstrations of low value' (DLVs), the former having the effect of raising social status while the latter has the effect of lowering it.

Of these qualities, leadership is the most animal in nature. Of the many dynamics which make up qualities of leadership, many are more animal and are equally relevant to the school playground or to a group of baboons as to a human scene! I would suggest that much of today's personal development writing, though it would make a good leader into a very good leader, would probably not work for everyone simply because the picture isn't complete. We need to take a look at the darker side of interaction to get the complete picture. This will give us some leads to follow in our quest for social status.

The main reason why pick up concepts are so relevant to status is because one of the basic assumptions made is that a woman will not be attracted to a man of lower social status, therefore most of the ideas talked about in this area are working on making sure that the man projects an image of being a high status male (most seduction gurus will explain the concept of how an alpha male will lead a group and enjoy all the perks of being a leader!). As explained, these characteristics are actually more general leadership qualities, and women too can learn from this animal scenario and can use a lot of the ideas to take more control of their lives, or to raise their level of respect from their subordinates at work, gaining greater self esteem and enjoying popularity which comes from social status rather than from being nice to people. So let's move on and start to see how we might apply this 'technology'.

There are six main variables in the way we can affect the way others see us, these are:
1. Our body language (posture, use of space, etc)
2. Our speech sound
3. Our language skills
4. Our inner self-feelings
5. Our appearance (body type, clothes, level of attractiveness etc)
6. Our facial expression

This list might be further simplified into appearance, speech and inner feelings
or: -

1. 1. Appearance; clothes, posture, body language, facial expression, body shape

2. 2. Speech; voice sound, articulation, language skill, knowledge
3. 3. Inner feelings; mood, attitude, self talk, comfort zone

We shall cover all of these with a view to giving you a complete makeover to become more respected and higher status, before talking in some depth about the psychology of certain situations, setting possible exercises and examples where it is appropriate. However, before we do this, let's examine the feedback loop.

When someone sees us they will form an immediate impression. If we smile, they might well smile back. Just as you enjoy people smiling at you, they also enjoy you smiling their way (sounds so obvious, but ...) If you appear to be in a positive and motivated state of mind, they too will feel 'lifted' when they see you (also putting you in a higher status position) If you look miserable and depressed they will probably try a little to avoid any kind of exchange (exception, very close friends), which will only make you feel worse (you will see them as being cold and unfriendly). If you walk around even pretending to be of high status you may well find your popularity and power increasing rapidly as others pick up on the subtle body language you automatically adopt, making them seek your approval and advice and making them want to follow your orders. So the point of all this is that THE WAY YOU SEE PEOPLE RESPOND TO YOU IS AS MUCH TO DO WITH THE WAY THEY SEE YOU AS IT IS TO DO WITH THEM . You cannot change people, but it is possible to do a lot to change the way they see YOU, and this will affect their behaviour towards you considerably. Remember that we are constantly communicating through our bodies, communicating our state of mind, our mood, our status and much more. As Bandler and Grinder (co founders of NLP) said ,'you cannot not communicate'.

A quick word here, we've all been in a situation where we've smiled at someone and they have apparently blanked us. You may have thought that they were unfriendly and probably felt that they enjoyed a rise in social status through blanking you (though the reasons for their not smiling could be one of many). On closer examination the power is more connected with confidence and strength of frame. Your attitude must convey one of unshakeable confidence and no emotional attachment to their response, this way you can frame the interaction as one where the other person 'missed an opportunity' to interact with you, and if done with conviction they might well work to 'get your attention' at some point because they realised too late that you were high status previously.

Back to 'you cannot not communicate'. As your first exercise, next time you go shopping, notice how the person at the till responds to different people as they pay. Notice how (assuming the person at the till is reasonably friendly) the mood changes so quickly from customer to customer. There are other dynamics at play too, particularly if they may know the customer or if they fancy them, or if the customer is particularly skilled at rapport, but as a rule you can see a rapid succession of changes between two random people and you can learn a lot through watching (discreetly and not for more than a minute or you'll be arrested!!). If the manager is called to help with a problem at the till notice the body language of both the manager/manageress and of the staff, noticing particularly postures and tones of voice. While you are out, experiment subtly, taking on slightly different moods as you pay, maybe pretend you are a millionaire and aim to project this through body language and voice alone. Really get into the role so you can see how just this subtle change causes quite a change in the nature of the interaction. Rather than just aiming to look more confident generally (which is probably what you have been doing up till now), experiment with a range of feelings and practise playing different roles. Be like an actor. By just subtly changing the way you hold your body and the way you speak, aim to come across as 'rich', or 'in charge' , or 'super cool,' 'popular' or arrogant/assertive. Have a good play and see just how good you can get at 'playing these roles' and drawing out different responses (maybe also experiment putting yourself in low status too, and make a mental note of exactly what you are doing and the responses you get) . You can gauge your success and skill at playing these roles through the kind of responses you get. Again to quote Bandler and Grinder 'the meaning of a communication is the response you get', in our case the level of response will indicate our level of success in our game of communicating our status.

As a flip side to this, some people may have physical limitations or features of a physical nature which communicate something which is not true. I knew a lady who had a natural posture which made everyone see her as being 'snooty', it was her natural body shape and posture. She had to spend a lot of time apologising for this, and often felt people took an instant dislike to her. Another young lad I knew had a very straight upper back and held his head very upright making him look like an arrogant trouble maker. He was actually quite a quiet and sensitive lad! When you see other people, how many assumptions do YOU make as soon as you see them? Go through your friends in your mind now and you'll probably find that a lot of assumptions have been made due to posture and due to the way people hold their bodies, and many of the assumptions really DO hold true, but not all. Now for the tricky bit. How do you think people see YOU? How many assumptions are they making when they see YOUR posture and the way you hold YOUR body? Maybe take a look in the mirror for clues.

So you can see how an awareness of this feedback loop can really help our self awareness. But what if we have been holding our bodies in such a way for so many years that we can't change our posture? Well yes, we do sort of 'set our bodies into position', but this can usually be corrected by certain exercises which we will discuss in the next chapter, exercises designed to free the body up and strengthen the muscles we need for great posture.

So, having looked at various little things and little exercises we can use for testing ourselves, we can now work on the many areas which we can develop to build a more effective self presentation. We have three main areas to attend to (appearance, voice and mindset) so we'll address each in turn.

CHAPTER 2

Appearance

Clothes

What we wear can hugely affect the way people see us. Women are as a general rule already very aware of this, and there is an old saying ' clothes maketh the man'. Let's set about seeing how much what we wear can influence how others see us.

It is no secret than women love a man in uniform. This likely relates more to the symbolic effect of the uniform than anything else. A uniform will elevate a man's status considerably. A police uniform will put a man in a position of being 'in charge' regardless of intelligence or other leadership qualities. Similarly a fireman's uniform will endow him with 'hero' status, both being 'in charge and having hero status are alpha male qualities! So, from our position of wanting to increase social power, where does that lead us?

Clothes can also convey impressions of wealth and of high self esteem. As talked about earlier we can see how at some level, any hint at wealth will trigger a mixture of respect, jealousy and a host of other behaviours (all behaviours which lower value) from other people (as mentioned earlier, curiously these feelings may generate attraction from them at the same time), so we can see how a good dress sense can make a massive difference when it comes to making a good first impression. Most people are already aware of clothes which make them look good, and an awareness of other dynamics here can be helpful. Are your clothes working on projecting wealth? Authority? Are they conveying that you are part of a group? Be totally aware of what you are projecting through your clothes. Women have the added complication of whether to use their sexuality or not. Female sexuality has huge persuasive power, although it is not a leadership quality!! Having said this, in addition to being persuasive to men, female sexuality does evoke envy and jealousy from other women, who may become a bit subservient to the 'alpha female'.

Posture

As already discussed, the way we hold our bodies will have a massive effect on the way people see us, and the way they behave in our presence. It is possibly the biggest one thing which can affect social power. I will give you some exercises and some checks you can do to test how you are doing.

Good posture not only makes other people more likely to consider us more socially powerful and attractive, it also will have a dramatic effect on the voice, which we will talk more about later. F.M. Alexander set about putting together the ' Alexander Technique'. Formed mainly for the benefit of actors, this works on posture to improve voice and stage presence.

During a day in our modern lifestyle there are many times when we are in a hunched over position. When we watch TV, when we drive, when we sit at a computer, I'd even put money on it that you are hunched over as you are reading this! What happens is that over time the muscles will become set into this position. The muscles at the front of your shoulders and the muscles at the front of your chest become shorter and become tight, pulling you head forwards, and pulling your shoulders forwards and actually restricting their movement so you might not be able to put them back where they should be even if you tried, and even if you can put them back the chances are that they will not feel comfortable in the correct position. In addition to the tightening of the muscles at the front, the muscles at the back will become longer and weaker. While all this happens to the top of our bodies, because of the sitting position, the muscles at the front of the legs become tighter at the top and your abdominals may become weak, so tummy or bottom might stick out a little as they are relatively unsupported.

If poor posture has been leaking away your personal power these following exercises could make a dramatic improvement in a short space of time leading to dramatic results. You'll look taller and slimmer and more attractive, people will take more notice of you and what you say. You will actually FEEL more confident! Interestingly people who sometimes stutter often see a great improvement as their voice becomes more powerful and the whole speaking process becomes easier, this together with increased confidence can result in a dramatic improvement in their condition. People will instinctively respond to you more, and their response will be one coming from lower status than before, putting you into higher status and making you feel more powerful as you speak to them. Overall your self-confidence will massively improve just with an improvement in posture.

There is evidence to suggest that the way we hold our bodies can affect the way we feel- if we are curled up it is hard to feel ecstatic, and if we have a big silly grin on our faces it can be hard to feel depressed, go on, try it ! When we adopt a good confident posture we can feel that confidence resulting from our internal response to the body positioning.

Okay, let's take a look at your current posture. Go to a full length mirror and stand facing it. Check your shoulders are the same height and your body is fairly straight. Also check that your weight is evenly distributed between both feet. If you are right handed you might often carry heavy cases on your right, which might make you lean slightly to the left, also maybe your right shoulder is higher than your left. This tells you that it's time you started using your left hand more to carry things in order to 'even things up'!

Now turn to your side and have a look at your 'side on' profile. Your hipbone should be over the mid joint of your foot, and your shoulders and ears should be in a vertical line directly above your hipbone. Your shoulders should be just slightly back, but looking natural and not looking 'pinned' back and ideally should feel nice and relaxed. Your tummy should be in and your lower back just neatly arched with your bottom looking neatly in place. If you can get your body to nicely stay in this position well done – remember what this position feels like and remind yourself constantly for the first few weeks until it feels natural, then periodically stand in front of a mirror and check again.

While you are stood in front of the mirror, play with your posture, let your head slump forwards, or totally slump your neck and shoulders forwards, then go back to your good posture and just notice how much better it feels and looks. Experiment striving to deliberately look low status, then deliberately looking high status.

The odds are that although you managed to find your good posture, it probably didn't feel comfortable. I'm going to set out some exercises to lengthen those shortened muscles, and strengthen those elongated weaker muscles, then I'll give you a few techniques for quickly checking your posture 'on the hop'.

Some of the exercises require a gym ball. These are particularly good as the additional work of the small muscles involved in balance and stability is even more beneficial to posture.

When the weak muscles are strengthened and the short tight muscles are lengthened you will find that your body will automatically assume good posture all the time

Stretching the tightened muscles

Hold each stretch for about a minute, and then gradually deepen the stretch as the muscles relax. You only need to do one type of exercise per muscle group!

Pectoral (chest) muscles

1.Wall stretch

Stand facing a wall and reach out with one arm and put your hand flat on the wall. Now turn your body away from the wall leaving your hand in position on the wall until your body has turned as far as you can turn it and you feel your chest muscle (pecs) being stretched.

Hold for one minute then repeat other side

2. Ball stretch

Kneel down on all fours, put one elbow out to the side on top of the ball and sink your body a little deeper toward the floor, till you feel your chest muscle (pecs) being stretched.

Hold and then repeat for the other side.

Upper Pecs and Lattisimus Dorsi

1. Wall stretch

Stand facing a wall and again put one arm out in front of you and put your hand on the wall, a little higher than last time. Keeping the spine straight bend over at the hips, your hand staying at the same place with your arm fairly straight until you feel tightness in your upper pecs and side, as the muscle loosens lower your body a little more to deepen the stretch .

Hold and then repeat for the other side.

2. With ball (stretch like a cat!)

Kneel on all fours, then reach out in front of you putting both hands on top of the ball and sink your body as low as possible until you feel a good stretch and hold it, sinking deeper when you can.

Hip Flexors

Kneel down on one knee, Supporting yourself with your forearm on the ball beside you. Stretch the front of your hip by pushing the knee on the ground backwards.

Hold and repeat for other side. This exercise can be done without the ball

Spinal muscles

1. Lie(on floor) on your back with your knees up (feet on floor). Keeping your shoulders on the floor, twist your spine by dipping your knees to one side, then other side and back again.
2.   Kneel down on all fours and raise your mid-back like a cat.
3. This also stretches abdominals!

Lie on your tummy, and keeping your hips on the floor. Hands under your shoulders and push your chest and shoulders up as high as you can.

These exercises will loosen those tight muscles which have been restricting your posture. Now let's set about strengthening those muscles which will hold your perfect posture in place. You can use a dumbbell in each hand, but when you start you will probably find that a can of beans in each hand is plenty!!

Do two sets of ten repetitions.

1. Reverse flye

Holding one weight in each hand, bend forward at the hips keeping the back straight and arms hanging down. Then raise arms out to the sides. This exercises the backs of the shoulders and across the top of the back- the muscles which will hold your shoulders in a perfect slightly back position.

2. Back raise

Lie over a ball on your tummy and raise the weights up to the front as you reach up several times. This can be done without weights or ball, just lie on the floor with your arms and legs fairly straight, then raise your arms up in front of you while you raise your legs behind. (ideally leaving just your tummy on the floor). You can also just hold this position for about a minute.

3. Crunches

Lie on your back with your knees up and hands on your chest and lift your head and shoulders and chest using only your abdominal muscles

These exercises will both lengthen the tight muscles which have been restricting your posture and will strengthen the muscles which will hold your perfect posture in place. One thing left is muscle memory- we want our body to remember exactly how this perfect posture feels so we can find it whenever we realise we have let it go and started to revert to old habits ! Here are a number of checks.

1. Find a full length mirror and adopt your perfect posture as described earlier. Hold it for a whole minute and then relax, but as you relax make a mental note of exactly what moves and how far you will need to move it to return to perfect posture. Practise finding perfect posture then letting it go until you can remember it and find it easily.
2. Flop forwards at the hips, letting your torso just hang freely, then slowly uncurl and straighten up vertebra by vertebra until you assume perfect posture.
3. Imagine you are a puppet and someone is pulling the string at the top of your head, let the string pull you straight.
4. Stand proud and straight, slowly turn your head to the left, and then to the right.
5. Bend at the knees, your back straight and against a wall, then leaning forward at the hips (back still straight) stand up slowly keeping back straight.

Bearing in mind that the way we hold our bodies is probably the first thing people notice when they see you, you can understand how important it is to get this bit absolutely right. Do it all with intelligence though. I have known personal trainers who overdo work on posture, both male and female. In the case of the female personal trainer the end result is okay, just, but they look a bit 'snooty'. In the case of a male personal trainer the end result is a look of arrogance, they actually begin to look like trouble makers even if they are completely placid people!! Naturally, for most of us there will be very little risk of this sort of thing ever happening! What we want to strive for is a look of confidently being in control of self and situation.

Body language

This is basically the natural communication of our inner feelings and attitude, together with numerous social signals which we learn to use as part of communication. There is a gender difference here in that generally women are far more skilled in both reading and using body language. In relation to personal power much of the important stuff was covered under the 'posture' section (good posture communicates authority, and the mind/body link would suggest that adopting a good posture can actually MAKE you more confident), but in addition we can add that a person in authority will tend to make slower movements generally (as true for the alpha male model) and is always unhurried and unstressed. People lower down in social status may spin their heads around and react more suddenly to a change in the environment. Also there is the issue of 'personal space'. A more socially powerful person might just tend to allow a slightly greater distance in an interpersonal interaction; it's as though they have a bigger 'aura' around them!

Also people in authority might appear to be more solidly 'rooted', having their body weight distributed evenly between both feet. Many claim this increases vocal power too as the body is balanced and able to use the breathing muscles more efficiently. Men being taught the art of seduction are taught that if a man adopts a wider stance and uses more personal space, women will see him as more 'in control', more of a leader and more confident, all of which are qualities relevant to social power.

One of the most important elements of posture is the position of the head. You can experiment in the mirror and you will see that the position of your head, whether your head is up or facing slightly down, can have a dramatic effect. If your head is right up (and possibly slightly back) when you speak you will look quite arrogant, if your head is in forwards and down position you will appear of little social importance. Experiment with this to make yourself aware of this effect; it is a MUCH greater effect on your impression than you imagine. You want your head fairly high to communicate social power and authority, while you want to avoid the arrogant 'confrontational' look!

Facial expression

As with body language, this is really just an expression of inner feelings and attitude, together with many learned social signals. However an awareness of how your facial expression works for you can be very useful, since facial expression is as much a part of communication as speech itself. Some actors spend hours looking into a mirror practising different expressions. I would never suggest anyone go this far but, maybe just look into a mirror and play a bit - have some fun next time you're in the bathroom !

Body shape

We all want to look our best, and generally this means looking as physically attractive as we can, but just for a minute let's talk about how our body shape affects our status.

Here I will give everyone a little comfort. Whereas no-one would argue with me when I say that a good body shape is attractive and as such will dramatically increase general social power, I will now say that a good leader or anyone possessing high social value will not necessarily have a good body shape. Social power is more linked to how you use your body and how you react to people around you than to body type. If you are in the presence of someone with a fantastic body, do not show envy or pander to them, as envy is a quality which will lower your social value (enhancing theirs!), and similarly if you pander to them you will be illustrating social proof to others that the person in question is of high status. Interestingly I can think of many short and slightly overweight men I have known who have been highly charismatic and very much leaders of groups, its almost as if their lack of vertical status is compensated in other ways. Similarly it is well known that in a group of women, fairly frequently the leader can actually be less physically attractive than the rest of the group.

Having said all this, I feel that at some level people with less attractive body types will always feel some envy towards those lucky people with fantastic bodies, so a good fitness routine will go a long way towards fixing this (particularly increasing self esteem), but just remember not to let that envy show when you're in the presence of someone with a fantastic body and you'll do well anyway in terms of social status.

Among male groups there is still a slight tendency for the 'best fighter' to be the alpha male, as he has the capacity to intimidate any member of the group, and also can offer protection for the others. Again, although the best fighter MIGHT be the gang leader, this is not always so by any means!

General attractiveness

Again, though not vital for social power, when you meet a group of people, who do you search for first? Probably the most attractive – looking good is high value in itself up to a point. As we all know, we can look our best and no better, but make sure you look your best at all times, and don't let on that you think someone is particularly attractive (verbally OR non verbally) as this again will transfer status and power to them.

CHAPTER 3

Speech

Here we come to the largest section. Remember how at school there was a loudmouth who just seemed to dominate every conversation? It was as if somehow just having that loud speech qualified them as the leader of the gang – all a bit barmy wasn't it! The irony of it is that they probably went on to greater success in adult life. I would guess that these people might have started to speak a little earlier in life than the others, and having had this head start they just stayed ahead of the others.

So yes, good speech is very much a part of the social value toolkit. Assuming there is no other impediment we can do much to improve this. When we speak of good speech we solely mean speech which is easily understood and speech which communicates effectively, as this is the purpose of speech. A person possessing a high level of personal power will always speak clearly and in a controlled manner (there is never any panic in their voice) and there is never any sound of great urgent dependency on the outcome of the conversation; as such the conversation will usually be unhurried and well delivered.

And so to work on your speech to give you this power too!

There are many things to deal with here. We have vocal sound and volume, the articulation, and how to respond quickly and clearly to get the words out. Furthermore we have language skill, and how well what we are saying communicates information and feelings etc. We also want to use our skill to be able to use words to communicate high value through knowledge, and finally we want the language skill to assert authority through persuasive language in social interaction.

In times when you have to be assertive, keep things under control – you can become very annoyed but you mustn't become angry. The person who loses control of themselves will lose control of the situation. (this is where we differ – in lower level society the alpha male character CAN get angry and assert his authority this way, however in 'higher class' society this sort of angry display will be seen to lower social value generally) . Using simple commands expressed forcefully is most effective; raised volume and clarity will increase the effect and level of compliance considerably.

Speech production

We have to look at two areas here, the mechanical act of producing the sounds (and getting them out quickly and easily), and the skill of putting your words together in a coherent and structured way.

Speech sound

Look over the section on posture, as good posture is essential for the most effective use of the diaphragm and breathing muscles used in good speech. Make sure that your shoulders are back and down and most importantly relaxed. Maybe swing your arms gently in an easy and relaxed way (like a pendulum) to check that there is no tension. Also check your chest and abdominal muscles in order to make sure that they too are completely relaxed. Speak a little and as you do, move your head forward and back and notice how the sound of your voice changes as you change your head position. Stand up straight and turn your head slowly to the left, then to the right then to the centre as you find ideal posture. Maybe let your head flop forwards pretending it is very heavy, then pretend it is as light as a feather and let it just float up to its ideal position. Make sure that your weight is evenly distributed on each foot and speak a little now, feeling relaxed. Enjoy the resonance of the sound.

Practise breathing from your diaphragm. Breathe out through your mouth by slowly tightening just the muscle around your belt to gently push the air out. Maybe pant a little using this same muscle to push the air. You could also maybe do a little 'Father Christmas laugh' in the same way

Another important bit, look at one corner of the room and say 'HA' then look at another corner and say 'HA' again, then go around the room changing focal points. This will give you good connection between breath and voice so you will be able to get your voice sounding at a moment's notice!

34

Practise varying your pitch, maybe by singing in the bathroom. Pay particular attention to those lower sounds getting them relaxed and resonant. Just sing something well known if you are being listened to!

The second part to the sound of our speech is the articulation, that is, our ability to get out the vowel and consonant sounds we need, so that no matter how quickly we speak we can keep our speech perfectly clear. There are a wide range of regional accents, so your speech sounds for the vowels and consonants may vary. However your main mission is to get your speech absolutely clear. As with any skill, practice will improve both the quality of your sounds and the speed at which you can produce them. There are four moving parts in speech, the jaw, the lips, the tongue and the soft palate, and we can train these to make the articulatory muscles stronger, more skilled and more precise! Remember, practice makes perfect.

For the jaw, there is little problem of weakness but there may be tension and restriction of movement, just practice BAH BAH BAH BAH until you feel complete freedom of movement.

For the lips (which produce P, B, F, V and W sounds) we could use these as exercises, maybe repeat each one three times.

> Piper Peter peeled paper
> Baby bob blows bubbles
> Fife feefee follows Philip
> Vivo Vinny velocity vole
> William warms wet windows

For the tongue (which produces sounds like T, D, Z, J, Sh, Th (think), Th (there),Y going front to back, also R in combination with lips and S) again we could use the following as exercises, maybe repeating each one three times

> Two teetering tots tutus
> Dodgy Dave diddles Douglas
> Zeezy zither zips zola
> James judge judges justly
> Shelly sure shames shows
> Theo thistle thinks thoughts
> Then those there
> Ranting Richards rearing road rage
> Yoyo yellow ya ya
> Sissy sister stirs sauces

For the hard palate (producing K,G, and Q)use these:

> Kevin catches kicking cats
> Gagging goggles
> Quentin queen quashes quarrel

Interestingly, the sound H is just a breath. However it can cause problems because it requires so much control. Practise this to test and improve control.

Harry haha hounds Horace horse

The vowel sounds require the mouth to take on different shapes to produce the varied resonances needed to produce the sounds.

I:	High sky nigh
Ow	wow how now
Aw	Saw warm storm
Ee	See eels glee
Oh	Oh no Joe go
Oy	Annoy joy boy
Ay	Stay away may hay
Oo	New duke's shoe
Ure	Pure Uria McClure
Air	Care bear's hair
Ah	Smarter hard car
Oo	Should good wood
Er	Worm learns words

If you go over these exercises you will become much more aware of how we actually work our articulatory muscles when we produce speech. If you wish to take it further you can find many tongue twisters on the net, or you could even get a voice coach. Clear powerful speech is very persuasive and you'll probably be surprised at just how much difference it can make to your life.

Finding those words

The next thing to deal with is the ability to find those words, both on occasions where you have to quickly come up with an answer and on occasions where you have to just speak and sound interesting. Bossy people will tend to just say the first thing that comes into their head and speak with the authority of ' knowing they are right'. They might speak complete rubbish but they speak with authority. Less 'forward' people will go through many more processes before speaking. What we can learn from this is that in a social setting (and to an extent in a business setting) it is usually a good idea to just 'let go' a little bit more and let your mouth just go. This way at the very least you have more chance of getting your say in before a decision has been made, and if you can say it with conviction and act with conviction people will follow YOU instead of Mr or Mrs Bossy boots. Also practise as many activities and games where a fast verbal response is required. Again remember 'practice makes perfect'.

The ability to just improvise a story is again one which just takes practice. A good place to practise this skill is when you read children bed time stories, or just practise making your account of your day as entertaining as you can when you catch up with your friend or partner at the end of the day.

Effective general communication with others

A lot has been written on this so if you've already read this stuff hold on and I'll aim to make it as entertaining as possible, hopefully I'll enlighten you with stuff you haven't read!

You've probably noticed that when some people talk to you, you become drawn in, you want to add bits to their conversation. Their conversation inspires you and you feel that the conversation is somehow 'enriching your life' .When other people talk to you, maybe some geek, they give facts and figures, and they often become excited because when they learned what they are relating to you they were excited and they think it will excite you, but you quickly become bored out of your skull as you feel you are receiving a lecture on a subject which really doesn't interest you at all. So why did the first person inspire you while the second person sent you to sleep? Maybe it's because the first person was speaking in a way which could draw in your own opinions and feelings and experiences, whereas the second person just fired facts and figures for you to attempt to memorise. There are many variables here; you want to have a conversation which ideally is about something which interests you, and you want to be able to give some input into the conversation. I once heard it said that 'no one really listens, we're all just waiting for our chance to speak'. I don't know quite how true that is because I think often people DO like to listen, but hey yeah, he has got a point hasn't he ? So maybe make sure that when you speak to someone you allow them room to include their thoughts, feelings and opinions, just to make sure they stay interested in what you're telling them!

Of relevance here is the work of Bandler and Grinder, the co founders of NLP. They studied the use of language as used by two highly skilled therapists; Vaginia Satir, who had a talent for digging right down to the roots of a problem, and Milton Erickson who managed to use very vague and open language in order to inspire people to search deep in their minds to find the solution to a problem. They devised a system for producing the effects of each therapist in turn, and they found that the two therapists were at opposing ends of a scale. Satir driving for detail and Erickson inspiring internalised searching by providing vague words which would steer thoughts in a direction without giving any great detail, enabling his client to go into a half awake trance while he/she applied his own meanings to Erickson's words to sort out his problem.

Specific   **Global**

Isobel-girl- person-human-mammal-animal-living-matter

Unsurprisingly this system is of great use to us. Good use of language commands respect, and when someone is glossing over facts, or trying to manipulate you or missing the obvious, you can use the system, looking at the end where we drive down for specifics to uncover facts, figures and details. If we want to use language which will encourage input through using vague language we can move to the language ideas relevant to Erickson. Great skill in this alone will make fantastic difference in your general communication skills and earn you respect. Do check out two books,' The structure of magic' and 'Patterns of the hypnotic techniques of Milton Erickson', both by Bandler and Grinder these will give great detail on this topic.

Okay so in a nutshell, Ericksonian language is as open as possible, and Satir would drive for detail.

Erickson: 'drive'   Satir:

Drive what?
Drive where?
What route?
Drive as in verb, or noun (road?)

In this example 'drive' is an unspecified verb, and 'Satir' is finding out all the specific details which are missing (deleted) from the verb. There are three basic language situations where we may need to use our skill in questioning:

1. Information deleted: Question using How? Who? Where? What specifically? Tell me more.

2. Generalisations: Question using these sorts of questions:

meanings to Erickson's words to s	Every single one
She always starts trouble	All of them?
I can't do it	Every time?
She never tries	Always?

What stops you?
What would happen if you discovered you could?

3. Distortion: (this is where the first bit of a sentence appears to make the second bit true-for example ' she keeps on looking at me funny so she doesn't like me' or 'I need a coffee, you'd better finish this off'.

Question using: How does X mean Y?
How do you know X equals Y?
Who says X equals Y?

Look these answers over. They are your toolkit for getting detail and driving right to the heart of a problem;

with a little adaptation they will also see off any verbal bullies who attempt to manipulate you.

Let's look at it in more detail

Simple deletion
- Important bits left out

I love it	Love what exactly?
I'm going out	Where are you going?
Are you ready?	What for?

Unspecified verb
- Details who, what, how left out

He upset her	How? What did he do?
Drink!	Drink what? How fast?

Unspecified referential index
Who? What?
-(those, them, they, it, her)

I've got bad feelings about this	About what? What are your feelings
They are helpful	Who are helpful? We don't like them.: Who are we, who are they?

Comparisons

-No details on what it's compared with

.:

:

Brian's faster than Steve	Faster at what? By what standards?
Sharon is smartest	Smarter than who?

Judgements (very common!)

He is bad	Who says?
She is nervous	You can't do that.

Nominalisations

Verb   Noun
Verb changed to noun eg educating - education
Stressing - stress
relating - relationship

.:

:?

We have bad relations	How are you not relating? (change noun back to verb)
I had poor education	What education did you have

These are the basic pattern for deletion which I hope will be of use and learning them you will feel more able to dig for information.

Okay, so now we've seen how we can be vague or specific, let's have some fun writing two accounts of the same story. One loaded with detail, one extremely vague.

First account

I went into town at 9.00 this morning, took the back route down Chell street, I went to the chemist to get some toothpaste and soap, then I remembered I was going to meet Dan in Harold's cafe for a coffee. We talked about his friend Steve and his work as an accountant. His salary is going to rise from 30k to 32k on September 24th.

Second account

I thought I'd go out this morning so I left quite early. Though I had a couple of things I had to do, I was excited about seeing a friend. He had told me he had had a few ups and downs recently. We met over a drink, and had a good catch up. He's doing so well, they are paying him lots and he's got a rise soon!

So which did you prefer, and which one gave you the most images in your mind? Have a good play, just make up a story and leave out as much detail as possible.

Let's now look at some tools used by bullies to manipulate people. These all form presuppositions, using key words and verbal structures to pre suppose the content to be true;

Mind reading (pre supposing your thoughts or feelings are known)

You know you can't do that!	Oh yes I can
You don't like me, do you?	What on earth makes you think THAT?
You must be getting full; I'll eat your ice cream!	No!

Cause and effect (as distortion) (challenge links between causing part and effect part)

You keep doing that you'll spoil it	Who says?
Seeing you has spoiled my day	How has seeing me spoiled your day?

Universal quantifier (generalisation) (all, everyone, never, everything,)

Everyone knows he's useless	Everyone? I disagree
You always leave a mess	Always? This is the first time and that's because I left in a hurry
You never sort the post	I seem to do it MOST days!

Tag questions (Won't you? Will you? Aren't you?) At end of sentence

It's your turn, isn't it?	No, I did it last time
You will lock up, won't you?	No, I did it last time.

(Notice that these are particularly manipulative. However, if used with a slightly different inflection, tag questions can sound like a request for approval or advice!!)

Adjectives – these presuppose what follows to be true

You're a good troublemaker	I'm not a troublemaker
You're a smooth con artist	I'm not a con artist.

Complex adjectives- (previous, New, Present, Old, Former, Last) (presupposes another time)

You did this the last time	There wasn't a 'last time'!

Repetitive cue words(again, too, either, another) these imply that you make a habit of doing something in a certain good or bad way, or they can imply you are like someone else who did something in a certain way.

You're not another failure are you?	No. Who failed before?

You can't solve the problem either	Did someone else try? Give me two minutes and I'll solve it
I don't like your attitude either	What do you consider wrong with my attitude and what else bothers you?

Quotes - these by-pass the system and the content is presupposed to be true

Example

Allan said you have to do the accounts	He hasn't said anything to ME yet
I've heard you are a bad driver	Who said? and on what basis?

Double binds -Give illusion of choice but outcome is presupposed

Example
(Presupposes you will arrange him a lift)

Have you arranged my lift for Friday yet or will you do it later?	Who said it was my job to find you a lift?

Time presuppositions (During, before, after, continue, stop, start, when, still, since – these function like adjectives)

Example

Are you STILL being difficult?	I wasn't being difficult in the first place

Comparative (deleted what subject is compared to) cue for this –as xxx as

example

(also presupposes Dave's unreliability)

If you're as unreliable as Dave we're in trouble.	Who says I'm anything like Dave?

Awareness predicates (realise, aware, know, notice, understand)(as with adjectives, these presuppose what follows to be true)

Example

Are you aware of the bad effect you're having?	Who says I'm having a bad effect?
I've noticed you picking your nose	I've noticed you doing it too!

Notice how any time related word or awareness word will function as an adjective and presuppose the accusation to be correct. Also watch out for quotes and be aware of comparisons and you'll be fine! This section is

VERY important. Make up as many of your own as you can think of to get a thorough understanding of how they work, maybe get a partner to make some up to throw at you so you can practise responding quickly too.

Another form of bullying is when a bully will attempt to fracture a person from a group by highlighting something which makes them different. This could be anything ranging from a physical feature, regional accent or dress sense to just an unusual point of view. The power of the bully rests solely on the level of response and a strong frame will identify to all that the problem belongs to the bully rather than the bullied.

Erickson not only left out detail, in his work as a hypnotist he would put in a range of presuppositions which served as empowering suggestions. We can use presuppositions in a   way to gently push an issue;

'I know you're thirsty, let's have a tea-break'.

'You children must be in bed either in 5 minutes or 10 minutes'.

'If you're as lost as I am we should ask for directions'.

'The boss said to turn back if we ran out of petrol'.

Look again at the presupposition patterns and see what ideas YOU can come up with.

He also used words such as 'could' and 'would' when asking people to do something. These serve to soften commands and are useful for all of us.

Example 'Can you lock up' becomes 'Would you lock up'.

So we now know how to dig for detail, how to tell a story in a way which will connect with people, and we know how to counter a verbal bully, all in all a pretty awesome set of language skills to have. This knowledge will give you greater credibility as you are impossible to manipulate, and popular as people really enjoy talking to you. A couple more pearls of wisdom which belong here. The human mind doesn't handle negatives at all well. Children find handling negatives even harder than adults. If you tell a child peacefully playing not to fight, they will hear this as a suggestion to fight! As adults, when we hear an instruction such as ' don't turn left' we have to think about turning left before we tell ourselves not to turn left. Each time we hear a negative we have to think of what the negative means to us first then find an alternative behaviour. Nouns have the same effect. If I said 'don't think of a yellow car' you would have to think of the yellow car first before telling yourself to think of something else. Similarly the sensory system - don't think of jumping into cold water (you felt that cold water before finding something else to think about)!!! When giving instructions avoid negatives and give nice clear uncluttered instructions.

The Word 'But'

Imagine you have a great piece of work which you bring to the boss/lecturer/teacher. They look it over and say ' yes you've worked hard and you've done many good things there but, you forgot to mention xxxx and you should have said something about xxxx .' ... how does that make you feel? The word 'but' somehow cancels the effect of all the positive things said before it, and you probably felt the lecturer was just 'buttering you up' ready for the criticism. What about if the lecturer had said ' yes you've worked hard and you've done many good things there and I wonder if you would like to give xxxx a mention, and possibly xxxx as well?' How does that make you feel? The main difference is that the word 'but' has been replaced with the word 'and'. Also notice that the first sentence used 'should' which implies no choice and implies that what was left out was essential to include, the second sentence offers the student choice (I wonder if you would like to … .?), which leaves the student more motivated.

The Word 'Try'

If you send someone off on an errand to get some milk, avoid the word 'try' as this word is a sort of 'get out' clause and may serve as an excuse for not getting it, they may come back and say ' well I did try but I was very short of time'. Had you said 'would you buy some milk in town' the odds of you getting that milk would have been much greater!

The word 'Why'

The word why is learned by children very early on and yields answers from exasperated parents so why should we avoid it? Somehow it causes a defensive reaction, maybe our parents use it on us in our teens. It sounds like the person using it is directly questioning you and/or your work/judgement. If there is a hold up and a long queue in a hotel and the manager goes to reception asking ' why is there such a queue' the staff might feel they were judged as being incompetent, whereas if the manager had used 'how', 'what', 'when', 'where' questions (example 'what is holding up the queue?') the response and following exchange would have been more productive.

The Word 'Because'

In experiments this word has a magical enhancing effect in persuasion as it implies that there is a reason behind your request, even if the actual reason given is completely naff. 'Can I have your seat because I've got an itchy neck?' is many times more effective than 'can I have your seat?'. The effect is because it implies a reason behind your request, though often not too much attention is paid to what the reason actually IS. So 'can I go to the front of the queue as I have a big day tomorrow?' might just fly!

The Word 'You'

We respond to various 'calls',(our name, our nick-name (s), various hand gestures, various noises, and the word 'you' when it refers to you in a special or pleasant manner) and the way we feel about responding to these depends on a number of things, but most particularly the context and our relationship with the person speaking to us. A telesales person might use our name and we feel this is over-familiar and a sales cliché, whereas if someone you feel attraction for uses your name it can be the sweetest sound on the planet. Nick-names have a fun element to them, provided we like them! A nickname can have a very 'private' and special feel to it, especially in a relationship context. People like being talked about in a positive way and the word 'you' is how this can be relayed. ' I hear you love pineapples.' ' I thought I saw you in the paper the other day.' Also if you're trying to tempt people it can draw them into your tempting picture. 'I know a place you would love. Tastefully decorated and lit, free Champagne when you go in, you love Italian food too don't you? It can also be used to elicit curiosity ('I thought I saw you up town?' … … - you didn't go to town and now you're curious about who was mistaken for you!). People like attention, recognition and affection, and it is for you to work out which 'call' would have the most appropriate effect at a given time.

Now let's turn to the world of seduction to glean some more information on personal power.

Just to quickly recap, we have two types of behaviours, those which increase social power (demonstrations of high value or DHVs) eg ' It's ok, I know the manager, he'll let you in for free' and behaviours which lower social power (demonstrations of low value or DLVs) eg ' I'll leave that tricky bit to you' or a nervous laugh. Just about everything we say or do will affect our social status, some things more than others (this is where posture and head position are vital). With regard to speech, we must say everything with strong confident personal conviction.

One of the most used techniques in seduction is to give a little tease, this is a very effective stealth method of DHV, though this has to be kept playful or resentment will store up to be released at a later time. In a seduction context, a little light teasing will lead to playful friendly banter. In a general social context you have to make sure that the other person is on the same wavelength, and a bit of light and playful teasing will serve to elevate your social status. It is best used as a little device for 'telling off' which flies under the radar, or it can also be used as a device for maintaining status if someone is slightly out of order and trying to boss you around. For example, Dave is a good worker, but has started loading crates of beer into the wrong lorry before receiving any instructions.

Boss could say:

'Dave, that lorry is supposed to be taking milk to the Prison. I know you've got mates in there but … … '

This is humorous, non confrontational and puts Dave in his place, also keeping the boss in high status. For the second example Ann is working in a shop as assistant manageress, the manager is a bit of a control freak and orders her to stack shelves as the people who usually do it are a number of staff down. Ann is of course obliged to follow orders ,though she feels the order is a put down for her, and rightly too.

Manager: ' Ann, go and stack the shelves because we're short staffed today. '

Ann: 'You're a cheeky sod asking your assistant manager to do shop floor work.Yeah okay I'll do it' (playfully said)

This is an under the radar light hearted way of telling the manager off for the put down. It subtly reminds the manager that Ann is an assistant manager and that the order is asking her to perform tasks outside of her line of duty. Although Ann has had to comply, and compliance is a DLV, she has done much to maintain high status value.

In a relationship context playful teasing can really do a lot to heat things up. As mentioned earlier, a woman will frequently 'test' a man, and a man must be ready to respond in a way which demonstrates alpha status, as she wants a man to show her that he is 'strong'. If a woman throws a question at a man which might cause him to qualify himself or give an emotional response he has to know that if he rises to the bait he will lower his value and fail the test. As women tend to only be attracted to males of higher status she will be less attracted to him. He can maintain or raise his status by showing no big reaction to the test, making 'no big deal' of it, or he can playfully tease her back, or he can be 'masterful', all of which will prove his worthiness and 'manliness' to her. If a man fails a test, the well known phenomena of 'nagging' can result, the easiest defence for a man is playful cheeky teasing. Let's have some fun looking at an example to see how these exchanges might run, and the underlying dynamics. First, what happens if SHE is eating a cake and getting it down her front and HE teases HER.

Man. 'You're such a messy eater, I can't take you anywhere, I ought to get you a napkin!'

She - just flirtatiously laughs

Here the man has cheekily lowered her value, which she responds to flirtatiously, attraction is high. But what happens if the situation is reversed, the man has cake down his front and she comments ' You're such a messy eater, I can't take you anywhere, I ought to get you a napkin'. Here the man is being tested. He is put on the defensive and the dynamics are completely different. If he qualifies himself he will lose value, if he does a silly nervous giggle he will lose value. This is a test, let's see what he might say!

Man. 'It's a very messy cake' qualifier, not good.

Man. Gets angry -emotional response, not good.

Man ' It's nice and I'm messy because I'm enjoying it' Humorous and playful but still a qualifier.

Man ' Careful sugar plum, your hair is falling on the icing of your cake' -assuming this is true, or even if it's not, she is put 'back in her box'.

Man 'Cheeky cow' -Playfully puts her in her place!

In way of summary of ways for a man to respond, I offer these, together with some playful responses a man could use.

1. Confident leader statements -'Well it had to be done' or 'Don't just sit there, give me some help.'
2. Comedy tease -'Please be quiet, you're making me deaf' or 'You talk so much it's a wonder either of us get anything done!' or 'be quiet, I'm working!'
3. Put her in the qualifying seat -'with heels that high I'm amazed you can walk at all' or 'That dog of ours needs feeding' or 'stop nagging and put the kettle on.'
4. Cheeky insult -'Have you got an off button' or 'Cheeky cow' or ' You are so rude'.

Examine the dynamics of these carefully. Notice that in the range of general conversation, both between partners and same sex conversational exchanges, the dynamics are essentially the same. These same principles can be used to make you more popular and they can raise your status. All generally best delivered playfully. In a relationship context women love playful teasing banter! However, whether in the context of a relationship or among friends, teasing must be playful since the minute it crosses the line and becomes more personal, resentment is stored up and the fun evaporates rapidly!

When we ask questions we can see some interesting dynamics going on. With regard to conveying high status or low status much depends upon the frame of reference, body language and voice tonality, but notice this. When we ask a question we are effectively channelling someones thoughts along lines chosen by US, (it's sort of a mind control thing which is very much part of everyday interaction), and so effectively they will be 'complying' with us as they provide an answer. Yes, compliance is a DLV on their part which will effectively put us in high status. Another possibility would be that when they respond, they might be feeling pleased to be giving you advice or information (putting THEM in high status as you are acknowledging their superiority in the chosen field) or alternatively they might feel the need to qualify themselves (DLV putting YOU in high status) . When questions are of a factual nature the response is more likely to be one offering advice (DHV on their part), but when the question relates to the person in question at a personal level it is likely to draw out a self qualifying reply (DLV on their part). Let's look at some examples.

You're with your boss at lunch time, a project needs to be completed by the end of the day.

YOU; ' So how many reports should I include to make it effective ?'

BOSS; 'Well, four would be okay, but five if you can.' (advice)

Boss gives advice putting him in high status.
This all connects up with another interesting psychology phenomena. When someone does you a

favour, notice how although you find them possibly more likeable you wont actually like them more (they are effectively acknowledging your high status, putting them in low status). When the boss is offering advice he feels he is doing you a favour and this will make him feel good but it won't necessarily make him like you more (you have effectively just confirmed his high status) .

YOU; ' So how is the football going? I heard you injured your ankle?'

BOSS 'Yes I had to take a week off. I'm gradually getting back into it now'

The boss has revealed a bit of personal information here and has some personal investment in the conversation (DLV). This effectively raises your status through lowering his.

YOU; ' So now your a married man/woman, what will be your next move in life?'

BOSS; ' Well first thing I'm going to buy a new house then I'm going to ... ... '

Here the boss will talk for hours about personal stuff (DLV)

YOU: 'What made you decide to go into law?'

BOSS; ' I guess I just looked around and saw where the good money was, then I had to somehow raise the cash to get qualified.'

Again he is singing his heart out here !(DLV)

YOU; 'So can you promise not to get into any more fights? It's so bad for the company image and you really are letting the side down. I know you're my boss but I'm very concerned'.

BOSS ' Yes I only lost control of myself because I was so stressed. I just couldn't help it. I'll try to control myself in future ... '

Massive DLV by the boss here which puts you very much in high status. He is both qualifying himself to you then making a promise (affirming YOU as boss here !).

This all relates to transactional analysis, to be discussed later. In the first exchange you were speaking from your 'child ego state' while the boss was in 'parent ego state' and in the final exchange YOU were very much in the 'parent ego state' and the boss was in 'child ego state'.

A couple of little ideas commonly used in sales , 'Double Binds' and 'Yes Sets' can be used to enhance your persuasive powers.

Double Binds

As discussed before, these give an illusion of choice. If a sales person wants you to buy something, rather than asking 'would you like to buy this' he will ask 'would you like this in blue or black', bypassing the question of whether or not you want to buy it. This is actually a presupposition; it is presupposed that you will buy!

Yes sets

Another sales device. The customer is given three (or more) questions, the first two having obvious 'yes' replies and the last question being a little more involved .

'You like it?' (yes)

'You can afford it?'(yes)

'Sign here.' (yes)

Another useful device is the use of certain words which people will respond to without thinking - if delivered with authority (or with the force of a command) they sort of by-pass the thought and reasoning process of the receiver because they are direct and because there is a bit of pressure to respond quickly. These are words like ' Stop' ,'Now' ,'Immediately' , also verbs deliverered as forceful commands such as ' Run' ,'Walk' , and little phrases like ' Do it now' , 'Sign here'. Maybe think of occasions where you might use these words and visualise yourself saying them and seeing the response. Mentally practise the tone of voice you will use to get the desired effect. This will get you more likely to apply them in real life situations. Bear in mind that if you overdo this sort of thing on any one person it might lose effect after a while, however the responses ARE hard wired in ! Think of any other verbs you might use and think of the context you would use them in.

Notice how this links up with the earlier talk about
the leader of the group being the first to make a decision.
When these commands are delivered, the person receiving
the command does not have time to reach a decision so
they will automatically follow orders. This is very similar
to the leader who in times when a decision has to be
made as a group, will get their decision in first and will
state it with force and authority, forcibly de-railing the
thought of the other members of the group.

These 'commands' can be very useful, but can
borderline on bullying. Salespeople sometimes use this.
They might have a contract they want you to sign (or
cheque) and they might just say ' sign here' as a command,
and you might just find yourself signing without thinking.
Having read this, you will be less likely to fall for this
slightly manipulative device now!

It's a good thing to convey that you have contacts
in high places and whereas must never brag (and this is
actually almost a needy behaviour and DLV- similar to
qualifying yourself) it might be an idea to let slip one or
two things which might just imply that you know people
in authority, or that you own a private jet, as long as it
is true!

One of the most important things in the case of
seduction is to be non-needy. This behaviour alone is
probably the single most important behaviour. If a man
gives a nervous laugh or if he nervously looks around for
his mates he loses value. Similarly if he shows extreme
attachment to the woman at any point of a relationship he
risks losing value. If he shows himself to be smitten with
a woman's beauty when they first meet, he will appear
nervous and needy and this too will lower his value. In

terms of social power there is a lot to be learned here. As shown in the earlier lists of alpha qualities, displays of neediness include any action which transfers power to someone else, (eg panic and seeking approval) this includes asking for advice, particularly if this is done in a way which might imply some dependency on the outcome. If you are seen to flatter somebody in a way which seeks their approval, this too is a DLV, as is any nervous laugh, or any laugh at something said by someone which is not funny enough to deserve a laugh!!

Any information which people will find of great interest or use can be given out as a DHV. If you know any particular information which is particularly relevant to the job someone does, or relevant to their social circle, this can be tantalisingly revealed as a DHV. Similarly, if you can drop in an idea you have which you've been speaking about to someone in authority, as long as the idea holds some interest for the people you are telling, the story will effectively be a DHV,

When you answer the phone, be sure to use a relaxed and resonant voice, as opposed to a high pitch squeaky voice and nervous hurried speech. I'm sure you can work out which is a DHV and which is a DLV!

In Tony Buzan's book,' The power of verbal intelligence' he points out that as a general rule, higher status individuals have a larger vocabulary. Think about this. There are many books out there designed specifically for the purpose of building vocabulary, and I do like Tony Buzan's work to this effect.

We can see that in speech and language there are many different areas where mastery would help to empower you. Probably the most important is to be able to make a decision and to express it quickly. Here practice makes perfect, but do the exercises on voice production to work on the mechanics and maybe go to a quiz where you have to verbally answer questions quickly and think on your feet on a regular basis. The second most important thing is to be able to defend yourself, and to have an answer when you feel you've been verbally manipulated. Go over the presupposition section thoroughly and make up lots of your own examples and think of where you might use them. Also practise the other tools which will all help you to become more entertaining and higher status!

CHAPTER 4

Mindset

This is all about the way you feel inside, and the attitude you choose to have towards those around you. Look back at the alpha male chart, and the playground gang leader chart here and you will get some idea of the real dynamics of animal leadership. The overall theme has been kept throughout the book that you want to have that overall feeling of control of the situation you are in through knowing that you can handle any 'challenge' put your way, and you will make sure that people will never see you as being needy.

An empowering technique used in coaching is to look at your self talk. There are several little things you can do here. Firstly always make sure that self talk sees a positive side to situations (work out exactly what benefits the situation brings even if on the surface the situation appears to be bad- a bad situation often carries with it a lot of CHOICE!), and let that inner voice talk to you completely in positive language terms, as the mind can't handle negatives (see earlier). Avoid telling yourself to 'try' to do something as the word 'try' implies possibility of failure – 'I will' is much more powerful. Choice is better than no choice, so tell yourself ' I can/ could/might do something' or ' I am able to something', instead of ' I have to/ought to / must/should do something.' Having any choice in doing what you do allows you to 'own' your decision which will make it so much more enjoyable, in fact if you use words like ' must', 'should', 'have to', 'ought to' it will feel as though you are being manipulated into something - by your own inner voice !!

Being empowered is largely about attitude. Your attitude has to be that you ARE the person you have so far been only TRYING to be. As so many books tell you, it's about the self talk, the voice inside your mind, get it to always say encouraging things to you, let it find the positive way to express itself at all times and let it empower you (inner self criticism will weaken your body language and your frame, - people will pick up on it and see you lowering your value , and when they see this they may even step in and attempt to raise their value by lowering yours even further!).

Part of the game is being able to present a cool, confident persona which is not easily shaken. To this end, if we get used to going outside our comfort zone on a regular basis we become accustomed to being in unfamiliar situations and keeping calm. Whenever an opportunity arises to do something new and exciting, and preferably right on the edge of your comfort zone, go for it. Can you think of what you might be able to do today? Tomorrow? Next week? In the near future? As you raise your tolerance of stress by becoming accustomed to stepping outside your comfort zone you will learn to avoid panic, which as we've mentioned before is a massive DLV, transferring power and status away from you.

Let's move on to how you might increase your value on a day-to-day basis, meeting new people all the time. You want to find a way to get people to look up to you. You want to be the person everybody wants to know !

Firstly, you don't have to agree with people. If you disagree the odds are you will actually increase your social value (you are showing strong belief in yourself). In fact it's likely that these people will want to talk to you more BECAUSE there is disagreement, and maybe they want to persuade you round to their line of thinking. They may well like you less yet want to talk to you more!! Use a little sensitivity though, we all know people who constantly play devil's advocate, and we all know how irritating this is!!

You don't have to get to know everyone personally, though in case of any personal conversations you can allow THEM to talk about issues they have feelings about, so long as you avoid getting involved and caught up in the EMOTION of the discussion. You may talk about the LOGIC of the discussion, showing sympathy and empathy and drawing a line at the point of emotional involvement. Showing an emotional reaction to something said is generally a DLV, especially if you get caught up in an argument with emotional content and you are arguing with emotion. (This is the general rule and not without the odd exception)

In any conversation your mindset could be that when you talk to people it is their privilege to talk to you, adopting this attitude will raise your social status, curiously making people want to know you more. However if you overdo this it could backfire as other people with strong personalities may find you irritating - the author knows of one individual who is so self-involved in this way the effect rings hollow and comes across as defensiveness/neediness! Think of people you know who are a bit 'up themselves' and carefully examine your feelings towards them. Notice how even if you have negative feelings towards that person you found it sort of frustrating that you couldn't communicate with them, and curiously this increased the desire to talk to them. (This is actually a technique used by 'pick-up- artists' who in a group situation will ignore their 'target' woman in order to generate attraction, then when they eventually pay attention to their target she will feel attracted and honoured).You can experiment with this attitude and then use your own judgement to gauge exactly how much of this attitude you would like to use. You probably already know people who have this attitude, so select someone you know who is like this and have fun imagining what it must be like to be them. Imagine yourself really taking on their attitude and body language and really dig deep to imagine the sort of things they will be saying to themselves and the thoughts they will be having as they speak to various people they know. Also imagine the sort of thoughts and feelings the people would have as they spoke to you, feeling honoured and maybe even a little nervous.

Another tool used by pick-up-artists is the 'false time constraint' (FTC). This is actually just the sort of thing the person in the above paragraph would do, as would a very important person who gives you the gift of a few minutes of their time! A skilled pick up artist when talking with a woman will convey that he might leave any second. He might tell the woman that he can only stay for two minutes, or he might just point his feet away from the target so it looks as if he might walk off any second. (When you give a time limit it cleverly makes it so it appears that THEY are taking up YOUR time rather than you taking up theirs, so putting you into high status). When giving a sense that you may imminently leave it makes the exchange with you a lot more valuable, making the person you are talking to work in order to make you stay a little longer. Again this is a rather manipulative technique, but I can right away think of a number of people I know who use it and are probably completely unaware of what they are doing. I'm imagining that if you're reading this, you are interested in people and love interpersonal interaction generally, but yes, an awareness and a little play with this will raise your social status in the same way it works for other people, and if used with discretion it will only serve to increase your status while allowing you to still remain much liked, but do it with awareness and with people in your wider social circle rather than with family and close friends. While I do stress a little caution, this is very much part of everyday interaction. I'm sure you've noticed how people talk more when you want to get off the phone and do things, or they keep you chatting up town when you're in a hurry! Next time someone imposes a time limit on you, maybe saying 'If you've got something important to say be quick, I'm on the way out!' be aware of your urge to speak quickly and be aware of how they are raising their value by lowering yours (you are taking up their valuable time). You might respond with 'yes, it is important but it can wait until you have more time'. With this response you are showing consideration, maintaining your value, and also arousing their CURIOSITY. It's quite likely that they will suddenly find the time to listen to you!!

Transactional analysis, as devised by Eric Berne in his book 'Games People Play ' suggests that as people we can function at three different levels.

There is still the CHILD part, which is the playful and fun part, which is very emotionally vulnerable. The child comes in two parts, the adapted child, which is the child behaving in the way the parents have instructed him/her, and the natural child which is wild and rebellious, but also highly creative.

There is the ADULT part. This is the part of us which functions logically, objectively and sensibly. This is the part we should strive to use all the time in general relationships, as you want to talk 'on a level' with your friends.

The PARENT part is the part of us which is modelled on our parents. This also comes in two parts, the part of us which is modelled on our parents own behaviour (unconscious copying) and the part which is modelled on our behaving the way our parents would have liked us to behave.

In different situations we can see ourselves adopting different ego states. When dealing with the boss we may go into a child ego state while the boss assumes his parent ego state, and the roles might be reversed if we have to 'tell off' a subordinate. Take a look back to the section on questions and see these two ego states strongly assumed in the first and last questions and responses. The two middle questions are closer to 'adult to adult' interactions, and feel altogether more like a friendly bonding type of conversation.

Think of yourself in different situations - when did you last adopt your parent ego state? Your adult ego state? Your child ego state? The odds are that you have been spending most of your time in your adult ego state which is good as this is the way we best connect with our friends. Does a mother-in-law or even a partner force you to adopt a child ego state on a regular basis? If so, this obviously isn't healthy; aim to steer your next interaction with them towards being an adult/adult interaction.

When a school gang leader interacts with members of the gang we can see a largely parent/child type of interaction going on, and ditto when we see a high status person interact with a lower status person. In fact the stuck up jerk we discussed earlier somehow also generated this parent/child type of interaction, so if you want to increase your personal power this would appear to be the direction to go. Aim to draw out qualifying statements and this should be enough to achieve the desired effect, hell why not, (only where you feel it's really okay to do this!). Adopt an bolt upright posture and look down your nose at them just to draw out the wanted reaction (best not do this with your friends though, the sudden change in your behaviour would seem very odd !).

In generating the Parent/Child interaction remember that you have to adopt the right mindset while also drawing out the right sort of responses from the person you are talking to. We'll include some exercises to help your mindset shortly, go over all the material about questioning, and maybe write down a number of questions you may use in a given interaction. With the knowledge you now have, assess each question in terms of DHV/DLV, also write down a set of possible responses that these questions might draw out.

Go through various previous interactions which you have had recently and remember as much as you can about exactly what was said and what responses you got from any questions you asked. Ask yourself what key questions were exchanged in the interaction. If you questioned them how did their responses affect the status values in the interaction? Could you have asked more effective questions? Did they question you, and if they did, did you respond in your child ego state? If this is the case, remember that if there were any situations where you REALLY had no choice but to respond in a qualifying manner, the most important thing when you respond is to not show any EMOTIONAL ATTACHMENT to your response, since an emotional attachment would make it appear that you are seeking approval (this will effectively lower your status). Another useful thing is to avoid using the word 'I' since if you use it you will own your response, whereas using more vague replacements will distance you more from your response. Let's look at an example: You were in town with your child, who wasn't quite potty trained and there was an accident in the supermarket. You bump into a friend later in the day.

Friend says: 'I hear there was an accident in the supermarket earlier; isn't Tommy potty trained yet?'

The question seems to demand a qualifying response which would put you into child ego state. Let's examine a number of possible responses:

You say: 'Well I've been trying to get him trained for months now but I just can't get him to stay dry. I've tried everything I know'.

This is weak. You have gone into child ego, and you even asked for advice at the end, all in all a massive DLV!!

You say: 'He has the odd accident, but he is getting better'.

This is okay, but it still feels as if you are qualifying yourself. So much depends on the frame of this response; if there is emotion in your voice you will sound as if you are qualifying yourself, whereas if you say this in an emotionally detached way you will hold your value well!

You say; 'Accidents happen, we all know this. How was YOUR day?'

Here it looks as if you have deflected any emotional response or qualifying response, but have you? Again so much depends upon the bigger frame, your body language, your tone of voice and facial expression. It could be said in a slightly angry way, or resigned way, both of which would be emotional responses and as such would cause us to lose value. If it was said with a smirk it would be better. However, if the reply was said with a dismissive and relaxed laugh our humour will completely save face and actually increase our value, since we have shown that we cannot be pushed into a DLV!!

This last point is actually very important. If you show that you can't be easily pushed into a DLV type of response you are in fact not just holding your value-you are actually increasing it!! In the seduction world, 'pick-up-artists' are taught that women will test a man in this way - throwing awkward questions at him, or throwing other tests at him which will potentially push him into a corner and force him to behave in a way which will lower his value. A pick up artist is told to watch out for these 'hoops' a woman may try to force him to jump through and is told to either answer back with a question or ignore the question completely, but at all costs to avoid the nervous laugh! Okay let's have another example: You were out driving and you were involved in a minor collision with another car, your friend says:

'I hear you had a car accident. What happened?'

You say: 'That's right. I was pulling out of the side road and I didn't see this idiot coming along the road too fast. I put the brakes on but still got the front of the car badly damaged'

This could be said with emotion as you 're-live' the experience as you tell them, this will be a massive DLV, it might even look as if you are trying to convince yourself that the other driver was at fault as you relate the story. If the same reply was said in slightly distant and confident relaxed manner (maybe a bit like a news reader!) the reply would be fine.

You say: 'That's right, no-one hurt thank goodness, but expensive! How did you do on your quiz night yesterday?'

Here we have avoided getting involved, (note absence of the word 'I') and we have fired back a question which may draw a qualifying response from THEM!

So you can see that the most important thing is to be cautious if we are asked a question (particularly a personal question, or one which may have an embarrassing answer) which might cause us to give an answer with emotional attachment. Obviously in some cases with people who are very close to you the rules are a little different, but when in a business or wider social circle social interaction you will see that this is often the way people appear to judge each other, so be friendly and open, but be cautious when answering loaded and baited questions !

Over to you now. You've been to town, people at work asked you to get some postage stamps, but you forgot. This is bad as whatever you do you have already lost value, how might you best respond when you are asked where the stamps are?

1. Apologise profusely.

2. Apologise and say you'll run back and get them now.
3. Say 'You've reminded me, oops. Yeah I'll nip out in the tea break'.

4. Say ' Oops you're right I've forgotten them but yeah I did promise, I could go out at tea break, but I am very busy. Does anyone else fancy a quick trip to town?'

5. Say ' Well it's not really my job, I was only doing you a favour. We can wait until tomorrow now'.

6. Say ' You're right, I've forgotten them, I did say I'd get them and we need those stamps now. Could you look after my desk for five minutes while I go out and get them now?

7. Say 'you're soo bossy. Yeah, you're right, we need those stamps. Could you look after the fort for five minutes, I'll go out and get them right now.'

Think carefully through the dynamics of the situation. A lot would depend upon your status in the office here, and the level of urgency for the stamps. Remember the most important thing is to not emotionally invest in the response. Also remember that going into child ego state and apologising profusely puts the other person into parent ego state, elevating their status. Taking control of a situation puts you into high status. Also you want to remain friends with the other workers. So both 1 and 2 are both putting you in very low status. 3 is better, but still a little low in status as you are effectively jumping up to perform a favour. 4 is better, with a bit of luck someone else will go and get the stamps, they will be doing YOU a favour putting you in high status. 5 is a very high status response which will work if you are the boss, but if you aren't the boss you might lose popularity (though you will actually be in high status!). 6 is taking control of the situation which is high status. Notice how saying ' could you look after my desk' is requesting a favour softly but forcefully. Had you said ' can you look after my desk? ' the effect is somehow weakened, even though the force of the command feels greater, (somehow the word 'can' sounds like begging, whereas 'could' sounds higher status) 7 sounds cheeky and humorous, yet being almost under the radar takes strong control of the situation.

If we want to feel socially empowered it can be of great help to know a bit about the way people work. For example curiosity is a powerful thing. If somebody has a secret, how frustrated can you get trying to get that secret out of them? If somebody you know is highly secretive and you feel that they are hiding something from you, you will do almost anything to find out what that secret is. If you want a response from someone who won't answer your phone calls, leave a tantalising message, maybe one that includes them, something like ' I thought I saw an article about your work place in the paper the other day. They described a person very much like you who was working for them. Looked like a very strange task they were talking about. And I just wondered if you'd read it too or if you knew anything about the project? I think you ought to know what they said about you!' You can see how in this situation the person will be eaten up with curiosity and even if they're trying to avoid talking to you, they will be pretty desperate to find out what was said about them. Now then, it's YOUR turn to be high status. A little secrecy will increase your status. In seduction it is well known that a woman likes a man to have a little mystery about him, this is for the same reason exactly. So now, man or woman, a little mystery here and there will raise your status.

Also of great importance is the way you respond to secretive people. If you desperately try to get answers out of them it only serves to lower your status (almost begging and massive DLV, similar to self qualification, again it is an emotional response!) so do not try to get answers. In truth a secretive person is probably intolerably boring and being secretive may be the ONLY way they can generate interest (have a good think and judge for yourself in frank and honest terms how much effect any answer they could give would have on you directly and on the world in general!). Instead build your response through offering them incomplete stories and having a reciprocal secrecy. This will put you into high status and if you do your job well with no emotional attachment they will probably eventually be freaked out, causing them to lose status completely.

In order to be at our highest status, mindset is very important. One of the problems we have is that the personality we have is one which has been built up over many years, and at the moment you probably have a great number of responses 'programmed in' , and in any stressful situation your automatic responses will take over. This is where a few NLP based techniques can come in handy, since these will give you a chance to' rehearse ' an important interaction. If you've already done these sorts of techniques, I want you to go over them again, but working on more extreme behaviour. You may already have some idea of how that 'most confident you ' might behave. Yes you've probably already seen some good results, but you've probably come along the road as far as you will at this point. If I can say my favourite Bandler and Grinder presupposition of NLP again at this point ' IF YOU ALWAYS DO WHAT YOU'VE ALWAYS DONE, YOU'LL ALWAYS GET WHAT YOU'VE ALWAYS GOT'. I love this quote!! While we're on the topic, examine all sorts of things you are doing in your life at this point, in how many areas have you got into the habit of doing things the same ways every time, and in what ways can you change them ? Write down a list right now of these things and possible changes you could apply, and start applying those changes as from NOW. A good place to start changing the way you socially interact would be to experiment applying new behaviours in these following NLP techniques. You could become very snooty, very arrogant, then for purpose of contrast you could experiment playing very low status, running around after people, always agreeing with people, and remember the nervous laugh! Playing extreme ends of the scale will give you a much more solid awareness of how the different behaviours work in a social context. These following techniques are based on the NLP techniques of Bandler and Grinder.

Modelling

If you think for a minute of somebody that you would like to be able to get along with, but for some reason, whenever you try, you find you are just 'on a different wavelength'. Really get a clear picture of them in your mind. Focus on every little detail you can see. Notice the way they stand and how they hold their body, notice the expression on their face, and read their deep inner feelings from it. Imagine their past and all the life experiences a person like this might have had, and feel these experiences etched deep in their being. Really dig deep into the very essence of what makes this person what he/she is now. Next, using this knowledge, imagine the sorts of thoughts they might be thinking, and dig deep, if you were them what would YOU be thinking? Now imagine their voice, directly linked to their mind and their thoughts. Hear their voice speaking their thoughts, going the same speed as them and thinking entirely along their lines. When you are ready, imagine stepping into their body and holding your body as they do, imagine having the same expression on you face and the same experiences in life. Now imagine being able to think their thoughts and to speak with their voice. Next, imagine them seeing YOU right in front of them. From inside them, what are your exact thoughts and feelings on seeing you? How would that person like you to be different in order to really connect with you? Now float out of their body and into yourself as they see you, and imagine adjusting your behaviour in order to perfectly connect. Now go back into their body, and see how much better they feel as the 'you' in front understands and connects with them perfectly. Now go back into your body and remember everything you have learned; it will help you next time you meet that person.

We can also use this technique to learn what makes a person confident, more effective, or a better communicator, exploring their mannerisms and learning as much as we can through exploring as much about the things which give them that particular quality.

In our general quest to find out what results extreme behaviour might get, let's look at that snooty person nobody likes but everyone wants to talk to!

Imagine for a minute someone really stand offish and snooty. Someone who is not particularly liked, yet strangely enough people feel drawn to them and want to talk to them. Really dig deep to get to the essence of this character, what qualities have they got which make people want to talk to them? Imagine for a minute that you are in a conversation with them. See how they stand when they talk to you, see how they hold their head, hear the slightly condescending way they speak to you, and notice how they may walk away any moment, and yet, or because of this, you are actually working to make them stay. When you have that image clearly in front of you, imagine what it would be like to be in their shoes. Imagine yourself standing the way they stand, holding your head the way they hold their head, hear yourself saying the things they say, hear yourself sound the way they sound as they speak, and imagine thinking to yourself the thoughts THEY would be thinking. What is it that draws people to this person? Really dig deep and imagine all the qualities this person would have as they talk to the you in front of you. Again, ask yourself, 'Why am I drawn to this person? What qualities would I have if I were them?' When you really feel you have got the essence of that attraction, imagine their body being replaced by yours, and see someone else standing in front of you. Imagine yourself speaking to like that snooty person to the person in front of you. Imagine yourself standing the way they would stand and holding your posture the way they would. When you are ready, come out of this alternative you, and just watch the interaction of you (as the snooty person) and the person you have chosen to give the gift of your time. Pay close attention to the body language of the two people, and the sounds of their voices. Listen closely to the masterly sound of that alternative you. Then when you have absorbed every detail of the scene you can see, once again float into the shoes of the snooty person and pay particular attention to the response of the person you are talking to. Really work out what buttons the snooty person is pressing to get this effect. Learn as much as you can about their behaviour from this and imagine yourself pressing the buttons to get this behaviour.. Now come out of this picture and sit back and just imagine all the behaviours you saw and imagine the effect they would have on people, and think of situations where you might like to apply this behaviour. Think over the entire experience and gather together all the knowledge you now have. Finally, imagine yourself in interactions where you would like to apply this knowledge, and really dig deep as you imagine all the things you would say, the way you would stand, the things you would think to yourself. Again listen to your voice as you hear that slightly uninvolved sound when you speak and notice how you hold your body.

Now you have enough information to experiment a bit with the knowledge you've now amassed in situations where you feel it would be appropriate to do so. Bear in mind that you may actually be over cautious, you might even be afraid to use this knowledge as it is all new behaviour and unfamiliar territory, so ask yourself frankly ' does it REALLY matter what this person thinks of me ? ' The odds are pretty great that all your life up to now you have been over nice, and bear in mind that the new behaviour will make the person you interact with see you as less nice but more attractive. Dig deep and look at the bigger picture now, feel your eyes opening as you wake up to more possibilities during social interactions and really examine the way people see you. Are you too nice? Think back to all your recent interactions and examine the way you think people really saw you. Now just for a minute think back to people you know who have used these behaviours on you, and closely examine your feelings towards them. Remember, these are the feelings other people will have as they talk to you when you choose to use these behaviours, and also realise that you have a choice. You will have many wonderful things about you exactly the way you are, and now you are developing new aspects - those people you have been modelling probably envied aspects of YOUR personality, and you must keep the special qualities that belong to you as you already are safe, as they are what make you special and unique.

In counselling there is what is called 'the empty chair technique', this is similar to the modelling process we discussed. In the 'empty chair' technique, people can offload to a pretend character who may have done them wrong, or who they cannot talk to for a range of reasons. It gives the client a chance to really explore the situation from all angles. This is similar to the NLP technique of perceptual position, which we will look at as a good way to get the most productive results out of a meeting, whether of a business or social nature. This time we will have three positions looking at the scene, namely yourself, the other person, and a third imaginary person, who you think has exceptional good judgement in situations similar to the meeting you will have.

1. Carefully examine your own position, examine your thoughts and feelings towards the other person (in second position). Examine exactly what you want to get out of the meeting -are you being totally reasonable? Are you prepared to be reasonably flexible?

2. In your mind, look at the person you are meeting who is in second position. Notice his posture and facial expression and imagine what thoughts and feelings he has towards you. Explore the outcome he wishes from the meeting and his reasons for wanting it, and the feelings he may have attached to the outcome. When you're ready, step into this person   and take on his thoughts, facial expression and posture, see the meeting through his eyes. See yourself across the room, hear the voice of 'you' over there, imagining how he will feel, and feel those feelings.

3. Step back into first position. How does it feel different knowing what you have just learned?

4. Now imagine a third person, real or fictitious, who you can respect and trust to make sound judgement. Imagine him/her an equal distance from you and the person you are meeting.

5. Step into this person and see from this third position both the 'you' on one side and the other person on the other side. Be very aware of his/her thoughts and feelings towards the two of you. What would he/she consider the best outcome

for the meeting? What does he/she consider to be completely reasonable and fair?

6. Now switch places, so that you BECOME that third person, able to make sound judgement. How do things feel different?

This process can be of great help if you are meeting someone you feel you don't quite 'get', let's examine how it might be used to help us become high status - Again we will assume a position as someone who is very high status even if they are not particularly liked!

Now imagine that you are sitting in a room, and sitting directly opposite you there is somebody you don't know yet. Imagine they are looking at you and feeling slightly nervous, and wanting your time before you up and leave. Imagine being in THEIR chair looking directly at you. What is it that they see in you which has this effect? Dig deep and work out what qualities you are showing which have this effect. Again examine the attitude, the voice tone, and the confidence which generates this effect. When you have found out as much as you can, come back into your own body and imagine yourself taking on all these new qualities, many of which will probably feel quite alien to you. Stick with it, even if you don't feel comfortable with the 'new you' which is coming out here. You're not becoming a different person, you are only expanding the range of behaviours you have at your disposal. Dig as deep as you can as you take on this 'new you'. Now float back into the person sitting opposite you, examine carefully their feelings and get them right on the edge of frustration as you examine what is happening. Listen to the 'you' speaking to you, and feel that frustration as you eagerly put a reply in before the 'you' possibly will vanish. Step outside the interaction now and look at it from the outside; see the 'you' in parent ego, and see the stranger in child ego. Really enjoy watching the interaction as you enjoy the power which this behaviour offers you. Step back into the 'new you' one last time and assess which of these new behaviours you have learned will serve you the best.

Again if I can emphasise, you are not becoming a different person, you are only enlarging your repertoire of behaviours and looking for a wider range of choices so that you can become more socially powerful and more socially savvy. Enjoy all of the power you can have as you adopt a 'parent ego' more.

CHAPTER 5

What else will increase my social status?

We have looked at a range of qualities here, let's 'zoom in' on the social status aspect.

We have now examined all the big qualities which make a powerful and sought after personality. These are largely the qualities of the leader in the school playground,   or the alpha male type leader. I'm now going to apparently contradict myself. As I pointed out, a leader of a group is not necessarily the person who can make the best decisions, but is likely as not the person who will make the fastest decision and express it with force which will 'derail' the other people who have not yet come to a decision. Also I said that the leader of a group is probably not the most socially adept individual in the group. Having said all this, one of the most important ingredients in the set up is self confidence, and one of the most effective ways to gain confidence is to know that whatever you are saying or doing is the right thing to be saying or doing. This will give you absolute conviction in what you say/do, and because of your strong 'frame' in the interaction, people will follow you. So to this end, knowledge IS power (note that in event of a challenge, a natural leader can potentially override you even though you KNOW that you are right). They may provide a very strong frame which might overpower you and override you! However, if you state your case powerfully and with a strong frame, maybe even backing up your decision with related information to increase the force of your argument (DHV), with your new power the natural leader should back down for you, and might be a bit humiliated. This will now, (as in the animal kingdom!) cause the others to turn to you as the new leader!!).

These people skills are also the skills which will give you more fulfilment in all your regular relationships, enabling you to understand more about what your friends are feeling in any given situation. I know that as a tutor I used to use the word 'but' when I was giving my students an appraisal of their work having no idea that the word had a de-motivating effect. It really didn't matter how much you buttered the students up, when they heard the word 'but' they knew that criticism was following and they would instantly forget all the nice things I had said before the word! These days in similar situations I avoid using the word 'but' and I substitute it with 'and', this keeps the effect of the good things you say and just builds on them to include how you can suggest they might work to improve things even more.

This book of course cannot give you the knowledge to be right in every situation where a strong decision is required, but many of these situations are people related. There are many times where advice is sought regarding the best way to handle a difficult individual or a tricky social situation. Knowledge is power and the more you are able to provide people with solutions the higher your social status will be, as knowledge will earn you respect. People based decisions are common and as such this makes knowledge of how people work a potential DHV in many situations. To this end I will briefly go through some of the most important stuff with regard to the way people work and general social intelligence. I highly recommend David Lieberman,' Get anyone to do anything', Tiegger and Barron 'The art of speed reading people' , Tony Buzan - ' The power of social intelligence', Robert B. Cialdini -' Influence. The psychology of persuasion, and Leil Lowndes -' How to talk to anyone'. Let's indulge in a brief discussion of some of the ideas thrown up by this literature.

First of all let's quickly get an idea of the various personality types as identified by Myers Briggs. Their system identifies four different scales along which a personality can be measured. Potentially a personality clash might happen if two people are at widely differing points along the scale. Let's quickly look at these scales and potential clashes.

Firstly, the most well known, the Extrovert /Introvert scale. Extroverts love being with people, they talk about lots of subjects in little detail, and they are fast and animated talkers, while introverts love time alone, talk about few subjects in detail and speak more slowly and generally less. An extrovert might see an introvert as secretive and distant, while and introvert might see an extrovert as confused and overwhelming.

The second scale is the Sensor/Intuitive, Sensors love detail, are down to earth and very practical, liking tried and tested ideas, thoughts following logical sequences, whereas an intuitive loves to be different, loves inventing, loves concepts rather than detail, and so their thoughts dart around randomly. A sensor might see an intuitive as confused, whereas an intuitive might see an sensor as unimaginative.

Thirdly, the Thinker/Feeler scale. The thinker argues intellectually, is assertive, frank and honest, whereas a feeler is tactful, may lack assertiveness, argues emotionally, is empathetic with a warm, friendly personality. Thinkers might see feelers as over sensitive, whereas feelers might see thinkers as cold and clinical.

The final scale is the Judger/Perceiver. Judgers are tidy, organised and punctual, they feel a relief when a decision is made, whereas Perceivers are untidy, disorganised and don't like making decisions. Judgers may find perceivers frustrating with their lack of organisational skills, whereas Perceivers may thing of Judgers as controlling. I can imagine that while reading this you right away have a number of enlightening moments! No personality type is viewed as being better than any other, it's just that we work in slightly different ways!

The next very useful information is from Robert B Cialdini who identified various ways in which we are influenced. Let's talk about some of these.

If someone does us a favour or buys us a present we feel obliged to return the favour-this is RECIPROCATION. In the retail trade samples are given out to make you feel obliged to buy a bigger item in return. A way to cancel the reciprocation effect is to request them a favour in exchange (in a retail store possibly ask for change or for a toilet!).

A leader is more likely to be seen as a leader if other people are already seen treating him/her like a leader. You are much more likely to buy something if somebody known to you has already bought the product. This is called SOCIAL PROOF.

People are more likely to listen to people they find likeable or people they find attractive. This is called LIKING.

People have beliefs about what sort of person they are, and what they would and what they would not do. If someone is able to persuade a person to change just a tiny bit, it can be a lot easier to persuade them to change in a much bigger way along similar lines. This is called CONSISTANCY. The smaller change serves as a lever for bigger change.

If a person is in authority, or has a uniform, or if a person is expert in a relevant field and sets about persuading us, we are more likely to listen to them. This leaves us open to deceit from imposters. This is AUTHORITY.

If something is in short supply we are more likely to desire it. Both in the case of a person you can't get hold of, (or a person who has given a false time constraint) or in the case of the 'last item in stock' at the shop. This is SCARCITY.

Run through this list again and think of as many examples as you can for each of the laws of influence. Think of times when people have used these laws to manipulate YOU, and think about times where you may think it appropriate to apply these ideas for your own gain (not with good friends as they will feel manipulated and will like you considerably less !!)

Time can have an interesting effect on persuasion, if you request a favour a long time in advance you are more likely to get a yes as the time for the favour will feel far away in the future.

First impressions count - and so do last impressions. People remember what is said and done at the beginning of an interaction and at the end of an interaction more than what is said or done in the middle. These are the Primacy and Regency effects. Men are told that a woman will judge if there is a possibility of a relationship with a man in the first ten seconds or so, and we all probably tend to judge people initially in a similar time frame, so make sure that when you meet someone you have a clear idea of how you want that person to see you. Also those first few seconds meeting with any person can shade the whole mood of the whole interaction. The regency effect means that our last impression will last for a while after the interaction. This means it is also a good idea to finish each interaction on a high note, maybe just saying something a little humorous to raise a smile as you part your ways. If you leave someone with a big smile on their face it might well stay there for quite a while!

Interesting tip from David Lieberman. If someone is lying, one of the main giveaways is the over-compensation in behaviour. Also, if you introduce some plausible but fake information into the false story you could see how the person deals with it. A pause or change in story will give away a lie. As he/she tries to integrate your fake information, you will see if it is indeed a lie!

For example if a cheating spouse gets back late saying that there was a traffic jam, the partner might say 'I heard about the traffic jam, but it was all over an hour before your journey'. The naughty partner might now say 'most of the jam had gone, but it was still pretty bad', this integration of fake information would imply guilt. The reply may also be punctuated with pauses as the guilty person invents their story and checks plausibility as they go along.

Other tell-tale indications of lying are:

1. Incongruence in communication. The facial expression might not match the words or might be sort of 'fixed' throughout the performance.
2. There might be a hint of a smirk, indicating a sort of 'liar's high'.
3. They show signs of relief after lying. Once they feel they have successfully lied they feel relief and may speed up speech or hand movement.
4. There is often obvious sign of stress as the liar performs. Showing in change of voice or some involuntary movement.
5. The communication when lying will differ from the communication when they tell the truth. Speech speed and tone may be different and/or choice of words might be a little unusual for the suspect. It is most useful to get them to answer a question where you know the truth will be told for comparison. (In the interrogation trade this is called 'Baselining').
6. Again I emphasise there will usually be a pause before the lie is told. This is because a lie is a mixture of truth and deceit, and a careful balance has to be struck as the liar measures what he is

going to say. Telling the truth requires very little thought and the reply will be more immediate and totally congruent.

7. If the suspect changes any details of their story guilt is most likely.

Other ways of catching them are:

1. Pretend you know a lot more than you do – almost "it's ok, I already know"

2. Involve another person – "who did you play golf with?"

3. Ask the 'next' question –instead of "did you go to London" ask "where did you park? It's so hard to park in London".

4. Minimise the crime –"it's ok, we all do these things, it's so easily done." "You haven't done anything bad really"

5. Accuse them of a greater crime so they confess the truth in the form of damage limitation

It is very important to realise that there is usually a reason for a liar to lie. Maybe they are afraid to face the consequences of telling the truth, or they want to protect someone, or maybe a child or teenager is afraid that a parent will over-react. This advice ironically has been of immense use to me personally. My girlfriend's daughter would consistently lie to her mother and to myself, sneaking onto the internet without asking, and not wearing her coat to school in extremely cold weather, lying to her mother that she had worn it. Her mother constantly felt lied to and deceived. One morning, with agreement from mum, I played devil's advocate and teamed up with the daughter saying "it's so important she has a coat she WANTS to wear"(the reason why she hadn't worn her coat had never been questioned), which resulted in mother and daughter bonding on a shopping trip. These days her daughter wears her new coat everywhere! Then later I said it was ok for her to use the internet so long as she sought permission (she had previously feared negative response!). The result of this intervention was a massive positive impact on the mother/ daughter relationship, and there is now the wonderful warmth of 'trust' between them. Though the daughter still tells me that I am a pushover(!!) I feel this story will illustrate the value of getting behind the reason for the lying, which will often lead to greater understanding and stronger relationships between the people involved.

When dealing with people who are important to you, spotting a lie is unlikely to help a relationship, whereas spotting the cause for the lie can transform a relationship. Having identified a potential liar it is often more productive to search for the reasons behind the lying in a non-emotionally loaded way – getting the truth out of a liar by harsh interrogation is not always the best course of action! Cultivate relationships where honesty and trust are values held on both sides. If a person knows it is hard to dupe you they will be a lot less likely to lie to you, resulting in them having greater respect for you.

Also some DHV style tips from Mr. Lieberman - complainers, ask what they would do in YOUR shoes. To gain information ask specific 'how' and 'what' questions (the word 'why' triggers a defensive response) In case of an argument drive down to specific details, and if you have to persuade somebody round to your way of thinking the best possible way to do it is to 'guide them to your side' ideally making it seem to them as if they came to the conclusion by themselves.

A couple of DHV tips from Leil Lowndes. If being questioned on a subject you really don't want to be drawn into discussion about, you can use the 'broken record' technique. Each time they repeat or re-phrase their question, just repeat a nebulous reply over and over, something along the lines of 'that's private business and not open for discussion'. If you repeat this a number of times, they will stop questioning and you will be left in high status. Had you responded you would almost certainly have lowered your status. Also from Ms Lowndes - avoid cliches (DLV) – they are so over used that people tend to groan inside when they hear them, and to make matters even worse the same people tend to use the same cliches! Also, don't unload baggage (DLV).

Another good tip from her is one which can be used to draw out conversation by repeating the last information they gave as a question. Here is this device being used in the field of counselling where it is very commonly used.

Them 'She always gave me a hard time'

Counsellor 'Hard time?'

Them 'Yes she would always criticise me'

Counsellor 'Always criticise you?'

Them 'Yes, whenever we went out'

Counsellor 'Went out?'

On top of all of these, we've all heard about the value of positive talk as opposed to negative talk . Negative talk will always tend to be a DLV, and quality positive talk almost always a DHV.

Go over the last three paragraphs over and over again. Asking 'how?' and 'what?' will significantly reduce emotional investment and involvement on both sides when awkward questions are being exchanged, and the broken record technique is a brilliant way to keep yourself in high status. Also DO avoid cliches and unloading baggage, they are big instant DLVs!!

Rapport

Rapport plays an interesting role in social power. When two people 'hit it off' together we see how they will copy each others' body positions, being totally unaware of doing this. At a party or a club we see this over and over again;- one leans in, the other leans in too, one leans back, the other copies again. Anyone working in the world of sales, counselling, or any other job where people skills are highly important will have been told about rapport and will be reasonably skilled at using it to make customers or clients feel more comfortable.

Rapport is used to generate the ' I've only just met you but I feel like I've known you for ever ' feeling, and someone trained in rapport will subtly copy aspects of a person's posture, body language or speech to generate that ' you're soo like me' feeling of closeness. There are many books which cover rapport thoroughly, but yes, here is a short list of things easily mimicked to generate rapport. Don't overdo it though or you will be caught out, and the aftermath that follows will not be good !

Movement, general speed of movement.

Posture, the way they are sitting or standing.

Gesture, copy if safe. If they only gesture when speaking, you only gesture when speaking also.
Voice tone/mood of speech.

Emotional mood

Rapport is a valuable tool for generating closeness. However a skilled artist at this can begin by following, and then may begin to lead the interaction as the other person unknowingly begins to copy THEM. At this exciting point, if you can get them to follow you it will mean you have got them to see you as having social value and they are now following your lead!

In keeping high status, there is a time for generating rapport, but there is also a time for breaking it. If two people are in close rapport and one person breaks it, the other person will suddenly feel like something has been taken away and will often attempt to regain rapport; this effects attraction. A high status individual will frequently break rapport.

Okay so you now know all about high value, and about the dynamics (at animal level) involved in a typical power play type scene, which is mostly a fun bit of 'jousting and banter' with a little more at stake than is apparent on seeing the exchange at surface level. We don't want to always play for power, we want to gain a wide circle of friends who we love and who love us. So, what do highly likeable people do?

Remember details

If a man forgets his lady's birthday there is always big trouble! I remember several very moving scenes from films where the man is declaring how much he loves a lady by revealing all sorts of details about her that he has noticed and fallen in love with, 3 men and a little lady and Madagascar 3 come to mind. People love you to recall little details from when you last met them and previous conversations, and something like 'is your dog's paw better after the accident with that bin?' will really show that you care. Many salespeople and politicians actually write down these sorts of details. If you have a job which relies on close bonds with people this might be an idea for you too. Conversely if you forget a detail which is important to someone they might feel a bit disappointed and even a bit miffed.

When in Rome ... .

If you have been abroad and you speak to the people there in their own language, notice how their faces light up. They love the fact that before you came to visit them you took the time out to study a bit of their culture. Similarly, if you mingle with professional people of a certain trade it can be a big plus to know just a tiny bit of their jargon and stories relevant to what they do. Just don't try to be too clever!

Ignore blunders

We all make mistakes and do an occasional 'faux pas', and we really don't like having attention drawn to us when we do. If someone, particularly someone higher up the corporate ladder passes wind, DON'T draw attention to it. If you must say something, say something with face-saving capacity.

Good conversation manners

In any conversation of a non technical nature there are a number of unwritten 'rules'. What it all boils down to is that people like to feel they are listened to and respected, and they don't want to listen to someone who wants to advise them how to run their lives. Also people want other people to listen to THEM and they don't want to listen to other people's problems or be 'one upped'. Everyone loves compliments and most people find repetition irksome. Let's talk about this in a little more detail.

When people talk they usually want to be listened to. What they are telling you is important to them so:

If you interrupt them they will feel 'cut off in mid flow' and they will feel that you aren't interested in what is important to them. So if you're listening to someone in mid flow, shelve the urge to mention that your dog has recently learned how to open doors and can now fetch the paper from the shop!

We all stumble on our words occasionally and how irritating is it if someone finishes off your sentences! Make sure you don't catch yourself doing it, it leaves the other person feeling belittled and irritated, and the odds are you've got the ending wrong anyway. On the other hand never DELIBERATELY allow people to finish your sentences, this is a big DLV as is saying something like 'You know what I mean' – both will just give away your status.

Don't talk over people. You know how angry and frustrated you get when someone does it to you!

Don't offer premature advice, as people often just want to offload and may well not want to be advised. Make sure you hear the COMPLETE story and then carefully judge the situation. If they really want your advice they will ask for it.

If they are telling you a story about an achievement or adventure, avoid that urge to butt in with a one up story. If they tell you about their cold and their long hard day don't butt in telling them your day was worse - they probably only wanted a little sympathy, and you have just stolen their thunder and now YOU are requesting sympathy from THEM! Also if they are telling you about their recent camping holiday, shelve the urge to tell them about your recent holiday of a lifetime - it really is best to keep it zipped on this occasion!

Don't judge people - it's always unfair to put somebody in a box, and they will resent you for it.

Gossip is bad news for everyone - keep away.

Compliments

We all love it when people say nice things about us, and compliments are frequently returned if we dish them out, making everyone feel appreciated and recognised. There are many ways to deliver compliments, let's look at a few from the range.

You can imply a quality to be complimented on by saying you wished you had that quality too, particularly at a given time. (presupposition pattern- comparison deletion)

Examples

'I wish I was fit enough to run to the shops and back in ten minutes like you.'

'If I had your eloquence when I gave that speech I would have got a standing ovation.'

'Of course you're too young to remember the first moon landing.'

You can also relay a compliment 'This new boss is so organised' or ' Compliments to the chef'.

You can offer gentle ongoing compliments to encourage good work. When you see someone working hard at challenging work, say something like 'You're doing a great job there' or 'Hey that's really coming on now' or ' that cooking smells good already'.

At the other end of the scale are those big compliments which make people beam inside. If someone has just had a big stressful performance, a speech, a concert, a display or some athletic feat, they will be buzzing directly after the performance, and this is the time to approach them with something like 'you were fantastic'. Strangely if you wait too long after the event you will come across as insincere.

In a similar category, if someone has something outstanding, maybe a physical feature or a special talent/achievement (especially one which isn't usually commented on which holds value for the person concerned) a big compliment can raise their spirits for a long time afterwards.

CHAPTER 6

Conclusion And Summary

Well we come to the end of this book. Go over all of the information carefully, look over the exercises. In a nutshell, here is a short summarising list:

APPEARANCE

Work out the effect of the clothes you are wearing. Dressing with class will convey manners, style, wealth and above all status

Check your posture is powerful. Keep your head well up. Move fairly slowly and be relaxed with no sudden movements.

Body shape is not of massive importance (although physical attractiveness is seen as high value) - What's more importance is your self confidence and that you are not seen to be envious of anyone.

SPEECH

Keep your speech always more relaxed and slower than people around you. If you have to be assertive be sure to always be in complete control of the situation, keeping speech clear and commands simple. Work on voice sound (posture related), and articulation and practise activities where a fast vocal response is required to improve speed of response. Look over language section, remember the sneaky DHV of playful teasing. Use questions to both increase your value and to lower that of the people you are talking to when you think it is appropriate. Always keep speech in positive terms; unloading baggage lowers your value. Express commands avoiding negatives, so people understand them with minimal processing. Look over and learn all the forms of questioning and all the presupposition forms to maximise verbal self defence and ability to spot where essential information has been left out or glossed over.

MINDSET

When you go about your daily life be aware that some people will judge you and others might accept you unconditionally, particularly friends. (But fellow men, do be aware that your girlfriend wants to see the alpha in you, so avoid neediness, self qualification and complaining if you want to keep her!).

Be flexible, you can be warm and sympathetic a lot of the time but when you feel that there is risk of judgement being made keep yourself fairly distant and remember that you are now high value. Remember that it really isn't important that everybody likes you, and that it is easy for someone to actually not like you but still want your attention and want to talk to you. You can be ever so slightly arrogant; remember that if you disagree with someone it will probably increase your social power even if you become less liked. (They will want to talk to you BECAUSE they disagree with you, and maybe want to persuade you) Enjoy the power of a larger repertoire of human behaviour!

Constantly remember the NLP presupposition ' If you always do what you've always done you'll always get what you've always got' and ask yourself 'What can I do differently in my life TODAY?'

I hope you find this book enlightening. Remember though, look after and be true to your friends! Hoping you will enjoy this wisdom as much as I do.

END

Made in the USA
San Bernardino, CA
11 December 2018